2002

A BOOK OF GRACE-FILLED DAYS

MARGARET SILF

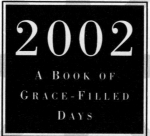

2002

A BOOK OF GRACE-FILLED DAYS

LOYOLAPRESS.

CHICAGO

LOYOLAPRESS.

3441 N. ASHLAND AVENUE
CHICAGO, ILLINOIS 60657

Published in Great Britain by Darton, Longman and Todd, Ltd. as
Daysprings
Copyright © 1999 Margaret Silf

Interior design by Kathy Kikkert

Library of Congress Cataloging-in-Publication Data
Silf, Margaret.
2002, a book of grace-filled days / Margaret Silf.
p. cm.
ISBN 0-8294-1643-9
1. Devotional calendars. I. Title: Two thousand and two, a book of grace-filled days.
II. Title: Two thousand two, a book of grace-filled days. III. Title.

BV4811 S3784 2001
242'.2—dc21   00-054591

Printed in Canada

01 02 03 04 05 / 10 9 8 7 6 5 4 3 2 1

INTRODUCTION

Jesus described his words entering our hearts as seeds falling to the ground. Some of these seeds are smothered by the distractions and preoccupations that seem to grow over our hearts as weeds take over a field. Some fall on our hard patches, which are impenetrable because of resentments or unresolved conflicts. Some are carried away on the winds of our distractions and our anxieties. Some, however, come to life and flower in fertile soil. These seeds take root in our hearts and experiences and continue to grow and come to fullness through our days, weeks, and years, transforming the very core of our being (Luke 8:4–8).

Yet how easily these life-giving words slip away and fail to germinate. When I find this happening to me, it helps me to remember the Samaritan woman of the Gospel who met Jesus at the well (John 4:1–30). He was a complete stranger to her, yet he knew her heart and he told her own story to her in a way that she had never heard it told before. She listened to the words of the one who is the Word, and those words became a spring of living water welling up inside her, flowing through her and making her life a place of joy and fruitfulness.

I believe that the words of Scripture hold that same promise for us today, two thousand years after that encounter at the well in Samaria. They have the power to tell us our own story and to connect our own life's experiences to the story of redemption. We are invited to listen to them and to reflect on what they might mean for us in the specific place, time, and circumstances in which we are living. Jacob's well is here and now, wherever we happen to find ourselves. The encounter with the Lord is today and every day, continually taking us by surprise and calling us to take one more step beyond ourselves and toward the kingdom of God. The living spring is ours to drink from and ours to share with a thirsty world.

2002: *A Book of Grace-Filled Days* is a little picnic basket to carry through the year. In this basket you will find a fragment of the living word for every day, together with a short reflection that connects the words of Scripture to simple events, thoughts, or encounters in our daily lives. Together, the words of Scripture and the words of the reflection offer you a space to spend a few moments of your own with the Lord each day. Sit with him a while at the well. Receive the seed of life that he offers in his words. Welcome the living spring that he opens up within your heart. Let him gently suggest connections between his word and your lived experience. And then take the joy and the vision you have discovered back to your own family, town, or community, just as the Samaritan woman took the good news back to her people centuries ago.

If you are familiar with the lectionary readings used in the Anglican or Roman Catholic traditions, you will find that each daily text is taken from the lectionary readings for that day. The full references for these readings are provided on each page, though there may be occasional differences between the various lectionaries. Whether your tradition uses a set lectionary or not, 2002 is an opportunity to be in prayerful communion with other Christians, as together we read and reflect on the word, which is God's gift to all of us. These fragments are small enough to carry with us through our busy lives. Yet because they are the word of life, they are big enough to nourish our hungry hearts and still leave us with an overflow of love and grace to share with others.

I would like to thank all those who have in any way helped me to put together this basket of fragments of word and prayer, especially my colleagues at Darton, Longman and Todd in London, and at Loyola Press in Chicago, and all my friends in North Staffordshire, for whom I originally wrote these daily reflections under the title *Potter's Clay*.

May you enjoy, day by day, the bread of God's word, grown from the seed of his love for you. May it nourish you and open up for you the living spring that is yours alone to discover, yet which flows from the heart of God, where we are all one in him.

*Be vigilant at all times and pray that you have the strength
to escape the tribulations that are imminent and to stand
before the Son of Man.*

— LUKE 21:36

I guard myself against drought not by filling up
my spare bottles with water but by remaining
close to the spring.

Daniel 3:82–87
Daniel 7:15–27
Luke 21:34–36

He shall judge between the nations,
and impose terms on many peoples.
They shall beat their swords into plowshares
and their spears into pruning hooks;
One nation shall not raise the sword against another,
nor shall they train for war again.

— ISAIAH 2:4

Liz smiled wryly as she recalled her student days. She had been radical, even violent, in her demonstrations against the injustice of the system. There had been a time for wielding the sword of protest, she reflected as she opened up the homeless shelter for the night, but now was the season for binding wounds, not inflicting them.

Isaiah 2:1–5
Psalm 122
Romans 13:11–14
Matthew 24:37–44

I say to you, many will come from the east and the west,
and will recline with Abraham, Isaac, and Jacob at the
banquet in the kingdom of heaven.

— MATTHEW 8:11

The hosts had carefully screened the dinner
guests to avoid social embarrassment. The
conversation was suitably polite and the
atmosphere a little chilled. Down the road at the
hostel the men shivered as they wrapped
thankful hands round bowls of hot soup; friendly
banter warmed up the raw night air. It was a
feast, because love sat among them.

Isaiah 4:2–6
Psalm 122
Matthew 8:5–11

Blessed are the eyes that see what you see. For I say to you, many prophets and kings desired to see what you see, but did not see it, and to hear what you hear, but did not hear it.

— LUKE 10:23 – 24

When we catch a glimpse of you in a baby's first grasp or an old man's memories, in the first crocus or the last autumn rose, we see what no book can contain and no human wisdom can reveal.

Isaiah 11:1–10
Psalm 72
Luke 10:21–24

DECEMBER 5

Behold our God, to whom we looked to save us!
This is the LORD for whom we looked.

— ISAIAH 25:9

A tremor of joy always ran through Jennie's heart
when she assisted at a birth. Every newborn
child seemed to be a carrier of the unspoken
hopes of all humanity. In a little speck of life was
a hope for a better future. How much more
powerful, then, is the hope that is born in you,
the bringer of eternal life?

Isaiah 25:6–10
Psalm 23
Matthew 15:29–37

Thursday

DECEMBER 6

• SAINT NICHOLAS, BISHOP •

Not everyone who says to me, "Lord, Lord," will enter the
kingdom of heaven, but only the one who does the will of
my Father in heaven.

— MATTHEW 7:21

My prayer ended, so I thought, with a heartfelt
promise to you that I would mend that strained
relationship. The real prayer began when I saw
her coming toward me in the street and faced
my desire to avoid the meeting.

Isaiah 26:1–6
Psalm 118
Matthew 7:21, 24–27

―――――――――――――

The LORD is my light and my salvation;
whom do I fear?
The LORD is my life's refuge;
of whom am I afraid?

— PSALM 27:1

When I stand in the full light of the noonday sun,
I do not worry about whether my flashlight
battery might fail. Then, Lord, knowing you to be
the ground of my being, may I let go of the many
lesser matters that pull me down into anxiety?

Isaiah 29:17–24
Psalm 27
Matthew 9:27–31

The holy Spirit will come upon you, and the power of the Most High will overshadow you. Therefore the child to be born will be called holy, the Son of God.

— LUKE 1:35 – 36

When your Spirit brings our hopes and dreams to life, they will surely grow into the fruits of your kingdom.

Genesis 3:9–15, 20
Psalm 98
Ephesians 1:3–6, 11–12
Luke 1:26–38

Then the wolf shall be a guest of the lamb,
and the leopard shall lie down with the kid;
The calf and the young lion shall browse together,
with a little child to guide them.

— ISAIAH 11:6

For two minutes the whole nation was silent, honoring the memory of their assassinated leader. At the graveside of this man who had lived and died for peace, his former enemies stood alongside his supporters while his grandchild spoke her simple words of love.

Isaiah 11:1–10
Psalm 72
Romans 15:4–9
Matthew 3:1–12

The desert and the parched land will exult;
the steppe will rejoice and bloom.

— ISAIAH 35:1

There is an inner desert where my branches fade
and fail in the heat of the sun and my leaves
wither. It is there that my roots reach down in
their great need for the untapped well of the
groundwater, which alone can bring to life the
hidden seeds in my heart.

Isaiah 35:1–10
Psalm 85
Luke 5:17–26

DECEMBER 11

A voice cries out:
In the desert prepare the way of the LORD!
Make straight in the wasteland a highway for our God!

— ISAIAH 40:3

When the Berlin Wall came down, most of it was
crushed to produce what turned out to be the
finest quality road-making material. The
roadblocks of oppression can be turned into the
stepping-stones of peace.

Isaiah 40:1–11
Psalm 96
Matthew 18:12–14

DECEMBER 12

For at the moment the sound of your greeting reached my ears, the infant in my womb leaped for joy.

— LUKE 1:44

Your greetings wait to surprise us around every corner of our living and in every moment of our days. And every time we recognize them, your life, growing in our hearts, leaps for joy and comes a little closer to its birth.

Zechariah 2:14–17 or Revelation 11:19; 12:1–6, 10
Psalm 45
Luke 1:26–38 or Luke 1:39–47 or any readings from the
Common of the Blessed Virgin Mary, nos. 707–712

Thursday

DECEMBER 13

• SAINT LUCY, VIRGIN AND MARTYR •

*For I am the LORD, your God,
who grasps your right hand;
It is I who say to you, "Fear not,
I will help you."*

— ISAIAH 41:13

Everyone could hear the hysterical sobbing amid the crowd of Christmas shoppers, but no one could quite see where it was coming from. Then the child's mother made her way through the mass of people, gently but with firm determination. She reached out to take hold of her toddler's hand. At once the sobbing stopped, and all was well.

Isaiah 41:13–20
Psalm 145
Matthew 11:11–15

⇒ 13 ⇐

DECEMBER 14

To what shall I compare this generation? It is like children who sit in marketplaces and call to one another, "We played the flute for you, but you did not dance, we sang a dirge but you did not mourn."

— MATTHEW 11:16 –17

I notice that my most desolate moods descend when the world won't dance to my tune or cry over my little troubles. I feel most at peace when I am so absorbed in another's music, or sorrow, that I forget to think about my own.

Isaiah 48:17–19
Psalm 1
Matthew 11:16–19

DECEMBER 15

Revive us, and we will call on your name.

— PSALM 80:19

We do not call on your name so that you might give us life. Rather, it is your gift of life, welling up inside us, that makes us able to call out to you, the source of everything we are.

Sirach 48:1–4, 9–11
Psalm 80
Matthew 17:10–13

⇒ 15 ⇐

DECEMBER 16

• THIRD SUNDAY OF ADVENT •

When John heard in prison of the works of the Messiah, he sent his disciples to him with this question, "Are you the one who is to come, or should we look for another?" Jesus said to them in reply, "Go and tell John what you hear and see: the blind regain their sight, the lame walk, lepers are cleansed, the deaf hear, the dead are raised, and the poor have the good news proclaimed to them."

— MATTHEW 11:2 – 5

When we see the life-giving power of your healing, we do not need to ask who you are.

Isaiah 35:1–6, 10
Psalm 146
James 5:7–10
Matthew 11:2–11

That the mountains may yield their bounty for the people,
and the hills great abundance.

— PSALM 72:3

The most fertile soil in the area had its ancient
origins in a volcanic eruption that had brought
devastation in its wake. In the same way, Lord,
our worst upheavals are often the source of our
richest growth.

Genesis 49:2, 8–10
Psalm 72
Matthew 1:1–17

DECEMBER 18

The angel of the Lord appeared to him in a dream and said,
"Joseph, son of David, do not be afraid to take Mary your
wife into your home. For it is through the holy Spirit that
this child has been conceived in her."

— MATTHEW 1:20

It frightens us too, Lord, and it can frighten
those around us when your seed starts to grow in
our hearts. Give us the courage to embrace your
deepest truths and take them home.

Jeremiah 23:5–8
Psalm 72
Matthew 1:18–24

DECEMBER 19

*He will . . . turn the hearts of fathers toward children and
the disobedient to the understanding of the righteous, to
prepare a people fit for the Lord.*

— LUKE 1:17

Turning back to you will always challenge us to
turn back to each other. There cannot be the
one without the other.

Judges 13:2–7, 24–25
Psalm 71
Luke 1:5–25

*Mary said, "Behold, I am the handmaid of the Lord. May
it be done to me according to your word."*

— LUKE 1:38

She gave you the blank check of her life. You
cashed it in. You took everything she had and
more and left her grieving at the foot of the
cross. And then you returned her capital with so
much interest that all the world could live on it
from that day forward.

Isaiah 7:10–14
Psalm 24
Luke 1:26–38

———————————

Blessed are you who believed that what was spoken to you by the Lord would be fulfilled.

— LUKE 1:45

Ben paused for a moment's rest after planting his spring bulbs. Only a bare patch of earth marked all his efforts. But he knew what would be there in the springtime. That knowledge—beyond sight and reason—transformed his labor and transfigured the bare earth into a place of faith and blessing.

Song of Songs 2:8–14 or Zephaniah 3:14–18
Psalm 33
Luke 1:39–45

*Once [Samuel] was weaned, [Hannah] brought him up
with her . . . [to] the temple of the LORD. . . . "I prayed
for this child, and the LORD granted my request. Now I, in
turn, give him to the LORD; as long as he lives, he shall be
dedicated to the LORD." She left him there.*

—1 SAMUEL 1:24, 27–28

The test of the purity of my prayer is this: when
you give me what I ask of you, can I immediately
let it go again? And can I do so with joy?

1 Samuel 1:24–28
1 Samuel 2:1, 4–8
Luke 1:46–56

*The virgin shall be with child, and bear a son, and shall name him
Immanuel.*

— ISAIAH 7:14 –15

Nothing would ever be quite the same again when the baby
was born. An entirely new and unpredictable stage of our
lives had begun, which was to bring difficulties, decisions,
heartaches, and great joy. This new presence in our lives
would, from this day forward, be with us in every moment,
waking and sleeping, and would change our lives
irreversibly. You too come silently into our hearts when the
time is right, changing us at our roots. Once you have
become God-with-us, we can never again be without you.

Isaiah 7:10–15
Psalm 24
Romans 1:1–7
Matthew 1:18–25

DECEMBER 24

The tender mercy of our God
by which the daybreak from on high will visit us
to shine on those who sit in darkness and death's shadow,
to guide our feet into the path of peace.
— LUKE 1:78 –79

To be in your presence is to become gradually
bathed in your light, as surely as to stand in the
dawn is to see the darkness melt into the
daylight. We can do nothing to bring your light
to our hearts. We can only wait and trust in your
promise of its coming.

2 Samuel 7:1–5, 8–12, 14, 16
Psalm 89
Luke 1:67–79

For today in the city of David a savior has been born for
you who is Messiah and Lord. And this will be a sign for
you: you will find an infant wrapped in swaddling clothes
and lying in a manger.

— LUKE 2:11–12

We wrap our gifts in glittering paper and adorn
them with ribbons, hoping to make what is
really very ordinary look like something special.
Your gift to us, your incarnate Word, comes
barely wrapped at all. You give us that which is
utterly special, but you wrap it in ordinariness so
that we won't be afraid to receive it.

VIGIL:
Isaiah 62:1–5
Psalm 89
Acts 13:16–17, 22–25
Matthew 1:1–25 or 1:18–25

MIDNIGHT:
Isaiah 9:1–6
Psalm 96
Titus 2:11–14
Luke 2:1–14

DAWN:
Isaiah 62:11–12
Psalm 97
Titus 3:4–7
Luke 2:15–20

DAY:
Isaiah 52:7–10
Psalm 98
Hebrews 1:1–6
John 1:1–18 or 1:1–5, 9–14

Wednesday

DECEMBER 26

• SAINT STEPHEN, FIRST MARTYR •

*But he [Stephen], filled with the holy Spirit, looked up
intently to heaven and saw the glory of God and Jesus
standing at the right hand of God, and he said, "Behold, I
see the heavens opened and the Son of Man standing at the
right hand of God." But they cried out in a loud voice,
covered their ears, and rushed upon him together. They
threw him out of the city, and began to stone him.*

— ACTS 7:55 – 58

As I walked through the barracks of Auschwitz-
Birkenau, I felt as if I were walking on holy
ground. In that place there had been those who
had joined their walk to death with yours. They
had walked through the jaws of hell and had yet
seen the gates of heaven.

Acts 6:8–10; 7:54–59
Psalm 31
Matthew 10:17–22

What was from the beginning,
what we have heard,
what we have seen with our eyes,
what we looked upon
and touched with our hands
concerns the Word of life.

—1 JOHN 1:1

He reached out to me in my distress, and my eyes met his. I saw the human friend, so completely familiar to me, but I saw too the mystery of the unknowable God, interpreted for me by his love.

1 John 1:1–4
Psalm 97
John 20:2–8

⇒ 28 ⇐

The angel of the Lord appeared to Joseph in a dream and said, "Rise, take the child and his mother, flee to Egypt, and stay there until I tell you. Herod is going to search for the child to destroy him."

— MATTHEW 2:13–14

"Where's the baby Jesus?" little Paul asked his parents, his voice full of disbelief as he gazed at the crib in the church on Christmas morning. The day had passed, dinner had been eaten, the new games had been played, and evening came. The family watched the news. "There's the baby Jesus!" exclaimed Paul with conviction, pointing to the pictures of a refugee family fleeing with their baby, the sound of gunfire at their heels.

1 John 1:5–2:2
Psalm 124
Matthew 2:13–18

[Simeon] took him into his arms and blessed God, saying:
"Now, Master, you may let your servant go
in peace, according to your word,
for my eyes have seen your salvation."

— LUKE 2:28 – 30

We recognize you when we welcome you and
touch your reality, and that happens when we
welcome each other and bless the Christ who is
at once both hidden and revealed in our brothers
and sisters. Such moments are blessed. They open
the doors to the peace that passes understanding.

1 John 2:3–11
Psalm 96
Luke 2:22–35

DECEMBER 30

• THE HOLY FAMILY OF JESUS, MARY, AND JOSEPH •

Let the word of Christ dwell in you richly.
— COLOSSIANS 3:16

Tangled up in all the conflicting demands of our lives, we forget that the richest treasure of all asks nothing more of us than to set aside a little space in our hearts where he may be at home.

Sirach 3:2–6, 12–14
Psalm 128
Colossians 3:12–21 or 3:12–17
Matthew 2:13–15, 19–23

DECEMBER 31

Let the heavens be glad and the earth rejoice;
let the sea and what fills it resound;
let the plains be joyful and all that is in them.
Then let all the trees of the forest rejoice
before the LORD who comes,
who comes to govern the earth.

— PSALM 96:11–13

In the last hours of the dying year our hearts and our homes break out in celebration to welcome the new. The winter trees are gestating the coming springtime, and you, Lord, are coming to claim us as your own.

1 John 2:18–21
Psalm 96
John 1:1–18

JANUARY 1

The LORD bless you and keep you!
The LORD let his face shine upon you, and be gracious to you!
The LORD look upon you kindly and give you peace!

— NUMBERS 6:24 – 26

A new year and another mile of the journey. Three hundred and sixty-five new chances to watch the sun rise on God's surprises along the way.

Numbers 6:22–27
Psalm 67
Galatians 4:4–7
Luke 2:16–21

⇒ 33 ⇐

JANUARY 2

*As for you, the anointing that you received from him
remains in you, so that you do not need anyone to teach
you. But his anointing teaches you about everything and is
true and not false; just as it taught you, remain in him.*

—1 JOHN 2:27

The touch of your truth on our hearts is the
reason why every falsehood within us leaves us
feeling exiled from our real home in you.

1 John 2:22–28
Psalm 98
John 1:19–28

If you consider that he is righteous, you also know that
everyone who acts in righteousness is begotten by him.

—1 JOHN 2:29

Clarry was the most cantankerous resident in the nursing home. Everyone kept out of her way. But one day she caught me unawares and insisted on showing me her photo album of the many stray cats she had once rescued and looked after. It was Clarry who taught me that God scatters his seeds in even the most neglected weed beds and grows his greetings in the most unlikely corners.

1 John 2:29–3:6
Psalm 98
John 1:29–34

*The next day John was there again with two of his
disciples, and as he watched Jesus walk by, he said,
"Behold, the Lamb of God."*

— JOHN 1:35 – 36

Let us be people who seek not to hold our friends'
attention but rather to redirect it toward you.

1 John 3:7–10
Psalm 98
John 1:35–42

Philip found Nathanael and told him, "We have found the one about whom Moses wrote in the law, and also the prophets, Jesus, son of Joseph, from Nazareth." But Nathanael said to him, "Can anything good come from Nazareth?" Philip said to him, "Come and see."

— JOHN 1:45 – 46

We would never refuse to unwrap a gift because we don't like the color of the wrapping paper. Why, then, do we so often refuse to get to know our neighbors, for no better reason?

1 John 3:11–21
Psalm 100
John 1:43–51

JANUARY 6

On entering the house they saw the child with Mary his mother. They prostrated themselves and did him homage. Then they opened their treasures and offered him gifts of gold, frankincense, and myrrh.

— MATTHEW 2:11

Carol paused for a moment and rested her hand on the head of her small son sleeping in the little bed. As she did so, she remembered the day. There had been a shaft of gold when his laughter had broken through the grayness of her anxiety. There had been a moment of true prayer when he had held his breath in delight as a robin hopped across the windowsill. There had been a time of pain and its healing when she had soothed his grazed knee and kissed away his tears. Gold for joy, incense for prayer, myrrh for healing. Gifts from a child. Gifts for a Child.

Isaiah 60:1–6
Psalm 29
Ephesians 3:2–3, 5–6
Matthew 2:1–12

Beloved, do not trust every spirit but test the spirits to see
whether they belong to God.

—1 JOHN 4:1

We can tell where a movement in our hearts or an influence in our lives is coming from by noticing where it is leading us. What comes from God will always draw the good out of our bad and the best out of our good. What is destructive within us or around us will always diminish our good into bad and our bad into worst.

1 John 3:22–4:6
Psalm 2
Matthew 4:12–17, 23–25

Tuesday

JANUARY 8

By now it was already late and his disciples approached
him and said, "This is a deserted place and it is already
very late. Dismiss them so that they can go to the
surrounding farms and villages and buy themselves
something to eat." He said to them in reply, "Give them
some food yourselves."

— MARK 6:35 – 37

"Why don't you save the millions of starving
children in the world?" I asked you.
"Why don't you drop in on the old lady next
door to see if she is warm enough?" you replied.

1 John 4:7–10
Psalm 72
Mark 6:34–44

JANUARY 9

There is no fear in love, but perfect love drives out fear because fear has to do with punishment, and so one who fears is not yet perfect in love.

—1 JOHN 4:18

We walk through our lives constantly looking over our shoulder in fear of expected pain and aggravation. How much more confidently we would move if we focused our gaze on the love that draws us forward.

1 John 4:11–18
Psalm 72
Mark 6:45–52

He unrolled the scroll and found the passage where it was written:
"The Spirit of the Lord is upon me, because he has anointed me
to bring glad tidings to the poor.
He has sent me to proclaim liberty to captives
and recovery of sight to the blind, to let the oppressed go free
and to proclaim a year acceptable to the Lord." . . .
He said to them, "Today this scripture passage is fulfilled in your
hearing."

— LUKE 4:17–19, 21

For two thousand years we have waited for your coming,
and every day we miss it because we expect it to come
tomorrow.

1 John 4:19–5:4
Psalm 72
Luke 4:14–22

*The report about him spread all the more, and great crowds
assembled to listen to him and to be cured of their ailments,
but he would withdraw to deserted places to pray.*

— LUKE 5:15–16

When I need you most, Lord, you sometimes
seem so far away. It is then, perhaps, that you are
in your lonely place, drawing from your Father
the strength for both of us.

1 John 5:5–13
Psalm 147
Luke 5:12–16

He must increase;
I must decrease.
— JOHN 3:30

The smaller I become, the less I weigh, the less I
am bound by the gravitational pull of my own
self-centeredness, and the more freely my soul
can fly to you.

1 John 5:14–21
Psalm 149
John 3:22–30

Not crying out, not shouting,
not making his voice heard in the street.
A bruised reed he shall not break,
and a smoldering wick he shall not quench.

— ISAIAH 42:2–3

Jane fought back the tears as her teacher reproached her loudly in front of the whole class. She wanted to sink into the classroom floor. Then she caught the warm, encouraging smile of her friend, and she knew that she would somehow find the strength to try again.

Isaiah 42:1–4, 6–7
Acts 10:34–38
Psalm 29
Matthew 3:13–17

JANUARY 14

Jesus said to them, "Come after me, and I will make you fishers of men."

— MARK 1:17

When we look at the nets that our own life story has woven, we see the holes of our sin and failure linked together by the threads of our faith and hope. Yet you use us as we are, with our faith and failure, our sin and hope, to make us into those who fish for your kingdom.

1 Samuel 1:1–8
Psalm 116
Mark 1:14–20

JANUARY 15

*All were amazed and asked one another, "What is this? A
new teaching with authority. He commands even the
unclean spirits and they obey him."*

— MARK 1:27

The fears and the temptations that haunt us in
our darkness are banished by the touch of your
authority as surely as a baby's nighttime terrors
are dispelled when his mother switches on the
light and takes him in her arms.

1 Samuel 1:9–20
1 Samuel 2:1, 4–8
Mark 1:21–28

Rising very early before dawn, he left and went off to a deserted place, where he prayed. Simon and those who were with him pursued him and on finding him said, "Everyone is looking for you."

— MARK 1:35 – 37

The solitude and silence of Kate's time of prayer was abruptly interrupted by an insistent knocking at the door. Her neighbor was in trouble and needed urgent help. "I'll come at once," she said, and she knew that her prayer had not been ended but had been made incarnate.

1 Samuel 3:1–10, 19–20
Psalm 40
Mark 1:29–39

The Philistines, hearing the noise of shouting, asked,
"What can this loud shouting in the camp of the Hebrews
mean?" On learning that the ark of the LORD had come
into the camp, the Philistines were frightened. They said,
"Gods have come to their camp."

—1 SAMUEL 4:6 –7

If, in the middle of my worst struggles, I can stop
and remember that God is with me in this
battlefield, then the warring factions in my heart
will shrink back, afraid, knowing themselves to
be powerless in your presence.

1 Samuel 4:1–11
Psalm 44
Mark 1:40–45

⇒ 49 ⇐

The rights of the king who will rule you will be as follows:
. . . He will take your male and female servants, as well as
your best oxen and your asses, and use them to do his
work. He will tithe your flocks and you yourselves will
become his slaves. When this takes place, you will
complain against the king whom you have chosen, but on
that day the LORD will not answer you.

—1 SAMUEL 8:11, 16–18

As soon as I allow anything less than you, Lord,
to rule my heart, it will drain me of all my
energy and my resources and make me its slave.
Only in my surrender to you will I be free, but
you will never force my choice.

1 Samuel 8:4–7, 10–22
Psalm 89
Mark 2:1–12

As he passed by, he saw Levi, son of Alphaeus, sitting at
the customs post. He said to him, "Follow me."

— MARK 2:14

If we follow you, Lord, we will find ourselves
walking alongside people we have spent a
lifetime trying to avoid, and we will forget why
we ever wanted to avoid them.

1 Samuel 9:1–4, 17–19; 10:1
Psalm 21
Mark 2:13–17

The next day he [John] saw Jesus coming toward him and said, "Behold, the Lamb of God, who takes away the sin of the world."

— JOHN 1:29

What a joy it is to discover something of the nature of God in his creation, or in music, or in our work, or in our human loves. But so much greater is the joy in following these signposts to the destination toward which they point us.

Isaiah 49:3, 5–6
Psalm 40
1 Corinthians 1:1–3
John 1:29–34

JANUARY 21

No one pours new wine into old wineskins. Otherwise, the
wine will burst the skins, and both the wine and the skins
are ruined. Rather, new wine is poured into fresh wineskins.

— MARK 2:22

Derek came in to school early to tidy the
classroom and prepare for the day's classes.
Before the children arrived, he wiped the board
clean of yesterday's work to make space for a
new day's discoveries. And as he did so, he
mentally let go of his preoccupation with his
own inadequacies. Yesterday's failures would be
no fit container for today's fruits.

1 Samuel 15:16–23
Psalm 50
Mark 2:18–22

But the LORD said to Samuel: "Do not judge from his appearance or from his lofty stature, because I have rejected him. Not as man sees does God see, because man sees the appearance but the LORD looks into the heart."

—1 SAMUEL 16:7

Marjorie took home a bouquet of the most expensive blooms from the flower show. Christine bought herself a dozen daffodil bulbs. The appearance is for today, but the heart belongs to tomorrow.

1 Samuel 16:1–13
Psalm 87
Mark 2:23–28

JANUARY 23

Again he entered the synagogue. There was a man there who had a withered hand. . . . he [Jesus] said to the man, "Stretch out your hand." He stretched it out and his hand was restored.

— MARK 3:1, 5

When I am feeling low, I nurse my sorrows as I do a broken arm and wrap myself in self-pity. I know of only one cure: to stretch out my hands and my heart toward a person who is feeling worse.

1 Samuel 17:32–33, 37, 40–51
Psalm 144
Mark 3:1–6

JANUARY 24

My wanderings you have noted;
are my tears not stored in your vial,
recorded in your book?

— PSALM 56:9

Little James didn't need to tell his mother about
all the sorrows the day had brought. He felt her
arms tighten around him, and he knew that she
knew and understood.

1 Samuel 18:6–9; 19:1–7
Psalm 56
Mark 3:7–12

Praise the Lord, all you nations!
Give glory, all you peoples!
— PSALM 117:1

We carry the light of the world in our hearts, yet
we often keep its release confined to a single
hour on Sunday, even though it so longs to spill
out over every moment of every day.

Acts 22:3–16 or Acts 9:1–22
Psalm 117
Mark 16:15–18

For this reason, I remind you to stir into flame the gift of
God that you have through the imposition of my hands.
For God did not give us a spirit of cowardice but rather of
power and love and self-control.

— 2 TIMOTHY 1:6 –7

Power without love can turn us into beasts.
Power with love can transform us into saints.

2 Timothy 1:1–8 or Titus 1:1–5
Psalm 80
Mark 3:20–21

Sunday

JANUARY 27

The people who walked in darkness
have seen a great light;
Upon those who dwelt in the land of gloom
a light has shone.

— ISAIAH 9:1

When I turn my back on the Light of my life, I
see only the darkness of my own shadow; but I
need only to turn, and the shadow will be
behind me.

Isaiah 8:23–9:3
Psalm 27
1 Corinthians 1:10–13, 17
Matthew 4:12–23 or 4:12–17

Monday

JANUARY 28

But no one can enter a strong man's house to plunder his property unless he first ties up the strong man. Then he can plunder his house.

— MARK 3:27

When I stifle the strongest yearnings of my heart, the lesser idols of my life take control. But when your sovereign Spirit reigns unhindered, the occupying forces shrink and withdraw.

2 Samuel 5:1–7, 10
Psalm 89
Mark 3:22–30

But he said to them in reply, "Who are my mother and [my] brothers?" And looking around at those seated in the circle he said, "Here are my mother and my brothers. [For] whoever does the will of God is my brother and sister and mother."

— MARK 3:33 – 35

We belong to the biggest family on earth. We are responsible for the loving care of a million siblings, and they for us.

2 Samuel 6:12–15, 17–19
Psalm 24
Mark 3:31–35

Go, tell my servant David, "Thus says the LORD: Should you build me a house to dwell in? I have not dwelt in a house from the day on which I led the Israelites out of Egypt to the present, but I have been going about in a tent under cloth."

— 2 SAMUEL 7:5 – 6

When we try to contain you, we are as far removed from your reality as a set of china geese fixed to a living-room wall is removed from the reality of the flight of wild geese that sweep the skies on their migration journey.

2 Samuel 7:4–17
Psalm 89
Mark 4:1–20

I will not enter the house where I live,
nor lie on the couch where I sleep;
I will give my eyes no sleep,
my eyelids no rest,
Till I find a home for the LORD.

— PSALM 132:3 – 5

A day without contact with you is a day exiled
from my innermost home; a night without your
blessing is a night without my deepest rest.

2 Samuel 7:18–19, 24–29
Psalm 132
Mark 4:21–25

This is how it is with the kingdom of God; it is as if a man were to scatter seed on the land and would sleep and rise night and day and the seed would sprout and grow, he knows not how. Of its own accord the land yields fruit, first the blade, then the ear, then the full grain in the ear.

— MARK 4:26 – 28

Nothing but the weight of our own imagined wisdom can prevent the secret, silent growth of your seed in our hearts.

2 Samuel 11:1–10, 13–17
Psalm 51
Mark 4:26–34

FEBRUARY 2

Now, Master, you may let your servant go
in peace, according to your word,
for my eyes have seen your salvation,
which you prepared in sight of all the peoples.

— LUKE 2:29 – 31

Every time we recognize the action of your love
in our world, the presence of your peace deepens
within us—the shalom of wholeness.

Malachi 3:1–4
Psalm 24
Hebrews 2:14–18
Luke 2:22–40 or 2:22–32

FEBRUARY 3

Blessed are the poor in spirit,
for theirs is the kingdom of heaven.

— MATTHEW 5:3

Susie watched delightedly as the soap bubbles
rose into the air. When she tried to clasp and
possess them with her small, eager hands, they
burst and vanished. But when she made no claim
on them and let them float freely, she saw in them
the reflection of all the colors of the rainbow.

Zephaniah 2:3; 3:12–13
Psalm 146
1 Corinthians 1:26–31
Matthew 5:1–12

A man from the tombs who had an unclean spirit met him. The man had been dwelling among the tombs, and no one could restrain him any longer, even with a chain. In fact, he had frequently been bound with shackles and chains, but the chains had been pulled apart by him and the shackles smashed, and no one was strong enough to subdue him.

— MARK 5:2–4

There are parts of me that I have buried so deeply that even I can no longer recognize them. There are aspects of my personality that I keep firmly fastened down with the chains of all my energy, for fear of what they might do if they break loose. But when the volcano erupts and the chains snap and my very worst breaks out, I find you standing there, ready to recognize me, heal me, and lead me to freedom.

2 Samuel 15:13–14, 30; 16:5–13
Psalm 3
Mark 5:1–20

He took along the child's father and mother and those who were with him and entered the room where the child was. He took the child by the hand and said to her, "Talitha koum," which means, "Little girl, I say to you, arise!"

— MARK 5:40 – 41

When you call us into the fullness of life, it is no solitary calling, but a miracle that affects everyone we love and everyone you love; your word, spoken to one, is spoken for all.

2 Samuel 18:9–10, 14, 24–25, 30–19:3
Psalm 86
Mark 5:21–43

FEBRUARY 6

• SAINT PAUL MIKI, PRIEST AND MARTYR, AND HIS COMPANIONS, MARTYRS •

When David saw the angel who was striking the people, he said to the LORD: "It is I who have sinned; it is I, the shepherd, who have done wrong. But these are sheep; what have they done? Punish me and my kindred."

— 2 SAMUEL 24:17

When our hands strike out against a helpless person, that dark moment will remain as a heavy shadow across an injured life, dimming the light for all around us.

2 Samuel 24:2, 9–17
Psalm 32
Mark 6:1–6

He summoned the Twelve and began to send them out two by two and gave them authority over unclean spirits. He instructed them to take nothing for the journey but a walking stick—no food, no sack, no money in their belts.

— MARK 6:7–8

No money can purchase an encounter with God, and no backpack can carry it. Only in our journeying will we experience it, when we are least expecting it.

1 Kings 2:1–4, 10–12
1 Chronicles 29:10–12
Mark 6:7–13

Herod feared John, knowing him to be a righteous and holy man, and kept him in custody. When he heard him speak he was very much perplexed, yet he liked to listen to him.

— MARK 6:20

The fear of the Lord allows us to recognize our own darkness, revealed by your light; it is the mystery that confounds our understanding yet irresistibly attracts us.

Sirach 47:2–11
Psalm 18
Mark 6:14–29

God said to him [Solomon]: "Because you have asked for this—not for a long life for yourself, nor for riches, nor for the life of your enemies, but for understanding so that you may know what is right—I do as you requested. I give you a heart so wise and understanding that there has never been anyone like you up to now, and after you there will come no one to equal you. In addition, I give you what you have not asked for, such riches and glory that among kings there is not your like."

—1 KINGS 3:11–13

If I ask you for happiness, health, success, and security, I am really asking you to enter into *my* kingdom. If I ask for wisdom and love, I am asking you to draw me into yours.

1 Kings 3:4–13
Psalm 119
Mark 6:30–34

You are the salt of the earth. But if salt loses its taste, with what can it be seasoned? It is no longer good for anything but to be thrown out and trampled underfoot.

— MATTHEW 5:13

The salt of our earth is packaged in fine silver salt shakers for the seasoning of our food, but it is also found in bins along the roadside for the thawing of snow and ice. We are called to awake in those around us the appetite for God and to melt away the barriers that hold them back.

Isaiah 58:7–10
Psalm 112
1 Corinthians 2:1–5
Matthew 5:13–16

There was nothing in the ark but the two stone tablets which Moses had put there at Horeb, when the LORD made a covenant with the Israelites at their departure from the land of Egypt.

—1 KINGS 8:9

When we enter our innermost self, we sometimes find nothing but bare space and the cold heavy stones of our covenant promises to faithfully remain in the place where we said we would be. Yet this same bare, painful, and uncompromising place is the place of the ark, where your Spirit dwells, making us ready for freedom.

1 Kings 8:1–7, 9–13
Psalm 132
Mark 6:53–56

Tuesday

FEBRUARY 12

• LINCOLN'S BIRTHDAY •

*Can it indeed be that God dwells among men on earth? If
the heavens and the highest heavens cannot contain you,
how much less this temple which I have built!*

—1 KINGS 8:27

It may take a lifetime to clear space in our hearts
for God. But can such space contain him? Only
if it is big enough to contain the smallest and the
most insignificant of his creatures.

1 Kings 8:22–23, 27–30
Psalm 84
Mark 7:1–13

*So we are ambassadors for Christ, as if God were
appealing through us. We implore you on behalf of Christ,
be reconciled to God.*

— 2 CORINTHIANS 5:20

The embassy offers sanctuary, guidance, and
support to those who seek it, in the name of the
power it represents. Can the same be said of us?
Do we offer hospitality to others in the name of
God's power and love?

Joel 2:12–18
Psalm 51
2 Corinthians 5:20–6:2
Matthew 6:1–6, 16–18

*For whoever wishes to save his life will lose it, but whoever
loses his life for my sake will save it.*

— LUKE 9:24

When we let go of the many lesser things we
cling to, we find we have empty hands to receive
the infinite more that you are waiting to give us.

Deuteronomy 30:15–20
Psalm 1
Luke 9:22–25

For you do not desire sacrifice;
a burnt offering you would not accept.
My sacrifice, God, is a broken spirit;
God, do not spurn a broken, humbled heart.

— PSALM 51:18–19

Nothing I can offer you is mine to give, Lord, because all is yours, and I give you only what you first gave me. All I can do is give you my own emptiness and ask that it might become a space where you can make your home.

Isaiah 58:1–9
Psalm 51
Matthew 9:14–15

The ancient ruins shall be rebuilt for your sake,
and the foundations from ages past you shall raise up.

— ISAIAH 58:12

Call us back, again and again, to the roots of
our believing—for if the roots are strong, the
branches will be sound and the fruit will be
life-giving.

Isaiah 58:9–14
Psalm 86
Luke 5:27–32

FEBRUARY 17

One does not live by bread alone,
but by every word that comes forth from the mouth of God.

— MATTHEW 4:4

If I had to live only on what I can see and touch,
what would I do for warmth, for air, for power?
What would I do for love?

Genesis 2:7–9; 3:1–7
Psalm 51
Romans 5:12–19 or 5:12, 17–19
Matthew 4:1–11

The law of the LORD is perfect,
refreshing the soul.
The decree of the LORD is trustworthy,
giving wisdom to the simple.

— PSALM 19:8

When I follow my own will, I may experience
pleasure and see the world through rose-colored
glasses. But when I follow *your* will for me, I
experience joy and see the world in its true
colors, illuminated in the clarity of your light.

Leviticus 19:1–2, 11–18
Psalm 19
Matthew 25:31–46

I sought the LORD, who answered me,
delivered me from all my fears.

— PSALM 34:5

I had a problem. I asked you for the solution.
You answered by releasing me from the anxiety
that was gripping me, and then, for the first
time, I was free to understand the real nature of
the problem, and there was space in my mind for
the solution.

Isaiah 55:10–11
Psalm 34
Matthew 6:7–15

FEBRUARY 20

When God saw by their actions how they turned from
their evil way, he repented of the evil that he had threatened
to do to them; he did not carry it out.

— JONAH 3:10

Miriam was trembling with suppressed anger as
she dismissed the class after challenging them
about their selfish behavior. Most of them walked
past her with their heads in the air and their eyes
defiant. But as Malcolm shuffled past, she noticed
the tears gathering in his eyes. He looked up at
her, distressed; her face softened into gentleness,
and he read forgiveness in her gaze.

Jonah 3:1–10
Psalm 51
Luke 11:29–32

FEBRUARY 21

LORD, your love endures forever.
Never forsake the work of your hands!
— PSALM 138:8

Our potter, of infinite patience and love, when
we are displeasing to you, do not cast us aside,
but take the clay of our hearts and mold it as you
would have it be, until it bears your imprint.
Your remolding will hurt, but it will not destroy.

Esther C:12, 14–16, 23–25
Psalm 138
Matthew 7:7–12

*And so I say to you, you are Peter, and upon this rock I
will build my church.*

— MATTHEW 16:18

You build a community of faith upon the rock of
our hearts and our lives, Lord. May that rock be
a stepping-stone for all creation and never
become a stumbling block.

1 Peter 5:1–4
Psalm 23
Matthew 16:13–19

So be perfect, just as your heavenly Father is perfect.

— MATTHEW 5:48

We are called to perfection, to completeness, to wholeness until all our fragmented parts are drawn together and all our brokenness is healed, until we are one in him and in his place.

Deuteronomy 26:16–19
Psalm 119
Matthew 5:43–48

Then Peter said to Jesus in reply, "Lord, it is good that we are here. If you wish, I will make three tents here, one for you, one for Moses, and one for Elijah." While he was still speaking, behold, a bright cloud cast a shadow over them, then from the cloud came a voice that said, "This is my beloved Son, with whom I am well pleased; listen to him."

— MATTHEW 17:4 – 5

There are wonderful moments in prayer when your presence embraces us with its power and its joy. Yet as soon as we try to capture and hold on to such moments, we lose them because we have switched our focus away from your reality and to the lesser reality of our own needs and longings.

Genesis 12:1–4
Psalm 33
2 Timothy 1:8–10
Matthew 17:1–9

The measure with which you measure will in return be measured out to you.

— LUKE 6:38

The living pool receives the streams from the mountains and lets them flow freely onward to the sea. The stagnant pool receives the inflow but has no outflow. The living water gives growth and life. The stagnant water diminishes into death.

Daniel 9:4–10
Psalm 79
Luke 6:36–38

FEBRUARY 26

[C]ease doing evil; learn to do good.
Make justice your aim: redress the wronged.

— ISAIAH 1:16–17

After the drunk-driving conviction, Jim had to
stop driving immediately. It took him a long
time to learn to live free of his addiction. And
then, very gradually, he discovered how to
channel his energies into helping those people
he had harmed.

Isaiah 1:10, 16–20
Psalm 50
Matthew 23:1–12

Jesus said in reply, "You do not know what you are asking. Can you drink the cup that I am going to drink?" They said to him, "We can." He replied, "My cup you will indeed drink."

— MATTHEW 20:22 – 23

Your cup is filled with many flavors, Lord: loneliness, fear, poverty, terror. But because your lips have touched it, it is always a cup of blessing.

Jeremiah 18:18–20
Psalm 31
Matthew 20:17–28

*Happy those who do not follow
the counsel of the wicked,
Nor go the way of sinners,
nor sit in company with scoffers.
Rather, the law of the LORD is their joy.*

— PSALM 1:1–2

It seemed churlish, at the time, when Jean kept refusing to watch the forbidden videos with her friends. She came close to losing their friendship, until they began to sense that she was the one person in their group to whom they could turn when the things they had seen on the screen started to take hold of their lives.

Jeremiah 17:5–10
Psalm 1
Luke 16:19–31

⋺ 91 ⋵

*The stone that the builders rejected
has become the cornerstone.*

— MATTHEW 21:42

Catherine was turned down at all her job interviews because of her debilitating handicap. Then her application for a disability allowance was rejected on the grounds that her handicap was not sufficiently debilitating. Trapped in this cycle, she turned to you. She learned to pray, and she prayed until her whole life became a prayer and many people came to her, seeking peace, wisdom, and *you*.

Genesis 37:3–4, 12–13, 17–28
Psalm 105
Matthew 21:33–43, 45–46

[T]he Pharisees and scribes began to complain, saying,
"This man welcomes sinners and eats with them."

— LUKE 15:2

We may learn to tolerate those who offend us,
but you show us how to *welcome* them. We may
bring ourselves to give them a meal, but you call
us to seek them out and share a table with them.

Micah 7:14–15, 18–20
Psalm 103
Luke 15:1–3, 11–32

*The LORD answered Moses, "Go over there in front of the
people, along with some of the elders of Israel, holding in
your hand, as you go, the staff with which you struck the
river. I will be standing there in front of you on the rock in
Horeb. Strike the rock, and the water will flow from it for
the people to drink."*

— EXODUS 17:5 – 6

The rock face of my most intractable difficulties
can become the source of your healing, life-
giving stream, but only if I can stand squarely in
front of it and claim its riches.

Exodus 17:3–7
Psalm 95
Romans 5:1–2, 5–8
John 4:5–42 or 4:5–15, 19–26, 39–42

Send your light and fidelity,
that they may be my guide
And bring me to your holy mountain,
to the place of your dwelling.

— PSALM 43:3

The winter sea was as black as the starless night.
A map would be useless in such a place, I
thought as I stood on the deck of the ferry.
Then, for a brief moment, the sweeping beam
from a distant lighthouse cut through the
darkness. We were still far away from the harbor,
but the direction was clear.

2 Kings 5:1–15
Psalms 42, 43
Luke 4:24–30

MARCH 5

In the fire Azariah stood up and prayed aloud: . . .
"For your name's sake, do not deliver us up forever,
or make void your covenant."

— DANIEL 3:25, 34

Every day you send us some reminder, small or great, concealed or obvious, that you are keeping your covenant promise to be with us always. And those reminders are what makes it possible for us to stay faithful to our covenant promise to walk with you.

Daniel 3:25, 34–43
Psalm 25
Matthew 18:21–35

Amen, I say to you, until heaven and earth pass away, not the smallest letter or the smallest part of a letter will pass from the law, until all things have taken place.

— MATTHEW 5:18

For as long as the river flows, it must respect the limits of its banks if its stream is not to become a destroying flood. Until the stream is poured into the ocean and the riverbanks have served their purpose, this is the law of its journey.

Deuteronomy 4:1, 5–9
Psalm 147
Matthew 5:17–19

*Whoever is not with me is against me, and whoever does
not gather with me scatters.*

— LUKE 11:23

Every moment of my life brings with it a choice
of how to spend that moment's energy:
gathering or scattering, with you or against you.

Jeremiah 7:23–28
Psalm 95
Luke 11:14–23

I will be like the dew for Israel:
he shall blossom like the lily;
He shall strike root like the Lebanon cedar,
and put forth his shoots.

— HOSEA 14:6–7

My short morning prayer, and the peace it gives
me, seems to evaporate in the hustle and bustle
of the day as rapidly as the dew disappears from
the grass blades at sunrise. Yet its effects
penetrate every moment of that day, nourishing
its roots and enabling its fruitfulness.

Hosea 14:2–10
Psalm 81
Mark 12:28–34

⇒ 99 ∈

Let us know, let us strive to know the LORD;
as certain as the dawn is his coming. . . .
He will come to us like the rain,
like spring rain that waters the earth.

— HOSEA 6:3

Barbara stopped by church on her way to work and knelt down before the altar, gazing at the east window, opening up her troubled heart in prayer. On the other side of town, Rahim stopped work for a moment in response to the silent prayer-call in his heart. He turned his inner eyes to the East and called out to the God of his fathers. Two strangers, two faiths, two human hearts set in the direction of the Lord and certain of his coming.

Hosea 6:1–6
Psalm 40
Luke 18:9–14

Only goodness and love will pursue me
all the days of my life.
— PSALM 23:6

The insurance assessor was unexpectedly
generous and considerate. The girl at the
checkout helped me pack my groceries, and a
friendly driver stopped and let me into the flow of
traffic. Your goodness and kindness is in theirs,
like a gold thread running through my day.

1 Samuel 16:1, 6–7, 10–13
Psalm 23
Ephesians 5:8–14
John 9:1–41 or 9:1, 6–9, 13–17, 34–38

You changed my mourning into dancing. . . .
O LORD, my God,
forever will I give you thanks.
— PSALM 30:12 –13

Maureen tried not to cry as she coaxed her small
son to leave her side at the start of his first day
of school. The fledgling fell so reluctantly out of
the safety of the nest because he had not yet
tasted the joys of flight.

Isaiah 65:17–21
Psalm 30
John 4:43–54

Tuesday

MARCH 12

Wherever the river flows, every sort of living creature that can multiply shall live, and there shall be abundant fish, for wherever this water comes the sea shall be made fresh. . . . Along both banks of the river, fruit trees of every kind shall grow; their leaves shall not fade, nor their fruit fail. Every month they shall bear fresh fruit, for they shall be watered by the flow from the sanctuary.

— EZEKIEL 47:9, 12

Your living water is no unsteady trickle, but an unstoppable river, flowing and overflowing with an abundance of life for us and for all who walk along our riverbanks.

Ezekiel 47:1–9, 12
Psalm 46
John 5:1–16

Can a mother forget her infant,
be without tenderness for the child of her womb?
Even should she forget,
I will never forget you.

— ISAIAH 49:15

Claire tried to pick up the pieces after her
teenage pregnancy and the adoption of her
baby. But for thirty years she yearned to know
the child she had given up. At last her lifelong
search ended with a long-delayed reunion and a
joy once lost but never forgotten.

Isaiah 49:8–15
Psalm 145
John 5:17–30

But you have never heard his voice nor seen his form, and you do not have his word remaining in you, because you do not believe in the one whom he has sent.

— JOHN 5:37–38

But those who do believe hear his voice across the marketplace and the factory floor and the playground, and see his shape in every human shape there is.

Exodus 32:7–14
Psalm 106
John 5:31–47

"Could the authorities have realized that he is the Messiah? But we know where he is from. When the Messiah comes, no one will know where he is from." So Jesus cried out in the temple area as he was teaching and said, "You know me and also know where I am from. Yet I did not come on my own."

— JOHN 7:26–28

My Stranger-Friend, I know you so well yet I don't know you at all. I know the part of you that shares my life and comes from my hometown. But there is a secret unknown part of you that comes from far beyond us both.

Wisdom 2:1, 12–22
Psalm 34
John 7:1–2, 10, 25–30

Some in the crowd who heard these words said, "This is truly the Prophet." Others said, "This is the Messiah." But others said, "The Messiah will not come from Galilee, will he?" . . . [The Pharisees] answered and said, . . . "Look and see that no prophet arises from Galilee."

— JOHN 7:40 – 41, 52

Why do we expect to find our Mother Teresas in India and not on the streets of our own neighborhood, when you have taught us to expect to find you where we are?

Jeremiah 11:18–20
Psalm 7
John 7:40–53

Sunday

MARCH 17

• ST. PATRICK'S DAY •

*He cried out in a loud voice, "Lazarus, come out!" The
dead man came out, tied hand and foot with burial bands,
and his face was wrapped in a cloth. So Jesus said to them,
"Untie him and let him go."*

— JOHN 11:43 – 44

Joe was seldom out of prison for more than a few
months at a time. The judges got used to his
continual appearances in the courtroom for
minor offenses. The truth was that he found
captivity a safer and more comfortable state of
life than freedom, and no one could free him
from his reluctance to free himself.

Ezekiel 37:12–14
Psalm 130
Romans 8:8–11
John 11:1–45 or 11:3–7, 17, 20–27, 33–45

⇒ 108 ⇐

MARCH 18

Let the one among you who is without sin be the first to throw a stone at her.

— JOHN 8:7

Lord, take the stones that we throw at each other in judgment and turn them into bread that we can share with each other in love.

Daniel 13:1–9, 15–17, 19–30, 33–62 or 13:41–62
Psalm 23
John 8:1–11

*Joseph her husband, since he was a righteous man, yet
unwilling to expose her to shame, decided to divorce her
quietly. Such was his intention when, behold, the angel of
the Lord appeared to him in a dream and said, "Joseph, son
of David, do not be afraid to take Mary your wife into
your home. For it is through the holy Spirit that this child
has been conceived in her."*

— MATTHEW 1:19 – 20

Whatever our plans may be, Lord, and however
well intentioned, keep our hearts always open to
the dream that is known only to you.

2 Samuel 7:4–5, 12–14, 16
Psalm 89
Romans 4:13, 16–18, 22
Matthew 1:16, 18–21, 24 or Luke 2:41–51

If you remain in my word, you will truly be my disciples,
and you will know the truth, and the truth will set you free.

— JOHN 8:31– 32

To make one small choice without fear of loss or
hope of gain is to make a choice in freedom and
to cast a vote for truth. And every vote will be
counted.

Daniel 3:14–20, 91–92, 95
Daniel 3:52–56
John 8:31–42

Jesus said to them, "Amen, amen, I say to you, before Abraham came to be, I AM."

— JOHN 8:58

To be who we truly are, fully and joyfully, here and now, is to *be* eternally, joined to the One who forever is.

Genesis 17:3–9
Psalm 105
John 8:51–59

In my distress I called out: LORD!
I cried out to my God.
From his temple he heard my voice;
my cry to him reached his ears.

— PSALM 18:7

We never allow our 911 lines to become jammed
by less important conversations. In the same
way, our cries to God override all our lesser
concerns and carry us straight to his heart.

Jeremiah 20:10–13
Psalm 18
John 10:31–42

Saturday

MARCH 23

*But one of them, Caiaphas, who was high priest that year,
said to them, "You know nothing, nor do you consider that
it is better for you that one man should die instead of the
people, so that the whole nation may not perish."*

— JOHN 11:49 – 50

"It is better to sacrifice the needs of a small
minority group, such as single parents or
unwelcome asylum-seekers, for the greater good
of the majority."
The words of our leaders, spoken to a nation
about to sell its soul.

Ezekiel 37:21–28
Jeremiah 31:10, 11–13
John 11:45–57

Who, though he was in the form of God,
did not regard equality with God something to be grasped.
Rather, he emptied himself,
taking the form of a slave,
coming in human likeness.

— PHILIPPIANS 2:6–7

Janice had poured her energy, her gifts, and her love into her work with the homeless and the powerless. In allowing herself to be emptied out, she made a space for you to flow through her life. She became a channel of love for many.

Matthew 21:1–11
Psalm 22
Isaiah 50:4–7
Philippians 2:6–11
Matthew 26:14–27:66 or 27:11–54

Mary took a liter of costly perfumed oil made from genuine aromatic nard and anointed the feet of Jesus and dried them with her hair; the house was filled with the fragrance of the oil.

— JOHN 12:3

When we respond from our hearts to your love and pour ourselves out to you in our prayer and in our living, the fragrance that is released will penetrate every dark and dusty corner of the world around us with unseen, unguessed power.

Isaiah 42:1–7
Psalm 27
John 12:1–11

Peter said to him, "Master, why can't I follow you now? I will lay down my life for you." Jesus answered, "Will you lay down your life for me? Amen, amen, I say to you, the cock will not crow before you deny me three times."

— JOHN 13:37– 38

When she got home after the service, Caroline was ready to give her life for the gospel. The phone rang. "Could you come over tomorrow, dear?" her mother asked. "I'm feeling really low." "Sorry, Mom," Caroline replied, "we've got an outreach meeting tomorrow. I'll try to get over sometime next week." As she put the phone down the clock chimed, shattering the silence and shocking her into a moment of cold, uncompromising truth.

Isaiah 49:1–6
Psalm 71
John 13:21–33, 36–38

Then one of the Twelve, who was called Judas Iscariot, went to the chief priests and said, "What are you willing to give me if I hand him over to you?" They paid him thirty pieces of silver, and from that time on he looked for an opportunity to hand him over.

— MATTHEW 26:14–16

What price would we sell you for, Lord? Thirty stolen kisses? Thirty careless words? Thirty angry thoughts? Sold to, and slaughtered by, the very lowest bidders.

Isaiah 50:4–9
Psalm 69
Matthew 26:14–25

He rose from supper and took off his outer garments. He took a towel and tied it around his waist. Then he poured water into a basin and began to wash the disciples' feet and dry them with the towel around his waist.

— JOHN 13:4 – 5

We will never find you in our Sunday service or in our Sunday clothes if we fail to find you in our weekday service, with our sleeves rolled up and our hands dirty.

CHRISM MASS:
Isaiah 61:1–3, 6, 8–9
Psalm 89
Revelation 1:5–8
Luke 4:16–21

LORD'S SUPPER:
Exodus 12:1–8, 11–14
Psalm 116
1 Corinthians 11:23–26
John 13:1–15

Pilate tried to release him; but the Jews cried out, "If you release him, you are not a Friend of Caesar." . . . They cried out, "Take him away, take him away! Crucify him!" Pilate said to them, "Shall I crucify your king?" The chief priests answered, "We have no king but Caesar." Then he handed him over to them to be crucified.

— JOHN 19:12, 15 –16

Richard's protest of the new management team's hire-and-fire policy was shouted down at the board meeting. "Don't you want to make this company a success?" they challenged him. "Are you with us or against us?" He sat down again, silenced, and the layoffs went on as planned.

Isaiah 52:13–53:12
Psalm 31
Hebrews 4:14–16; 5:7–9
John 18:1–19:42

Saturday
MARCH 30

• HOLY SATURDAY •

He has been raised from the dead, and he is going before you to Galilee;
there you will see him.

— MATTHEW 28:7

The group of pilgrims found a simple inscription above the
entrance to an empty cave in a garden in Jerusalem: "He is
not here. He is risen." It could also have said: "Go back in
peace to where you came from. And that is where you will
find him."

Genesis 1:1–2:2 or 1:1, 26–31
Psalm 104 or Psalm 33
Genesis 22:1–18 or 22:1–2, 9–13, 15–18
Psalm 16
Exodus 14:15–15:1
Isaiah 54:5–14; 55:1–11
Psalm 30

Baruch 3:9–15, 32–4:4
Psalm 19
Ezekiel 36:16–28
Psalms 42; 43 or Isaiah 12:2–6, or Psalm 51
Romans 6:3–11
Psalm 118
Matthew 28:1–10

So she ran and went to Simon Peter and to the other disciple whom Jesus loved, and told them, "They have taken the Lord from the tomb, and we don't know where they put him." So Peter and the other disciple went out and came to the tomb. They both ran, but the other disciple ran faster than Peter and arrived at the tomb first; he bent down and saw the burial cloths there, but did not go in. When Simon Peter arrived after him, he went into the tomb and saw the burial cloths there, and the cloth that had covered his head, not with the burial cloths but rolled up in a separate place. Then the other disciple also went in, the one who had arrived at the tomb first, and he saw and believed.

— JOHN 20:2 – 8

We search for you, but all we can find is the space in which we had tried to contain you. "You are looking for me in places of death," you tell us. "But I am the Life you can never contain within a fixed idea."

Our world seems like a dark tomb too, Lord, and all we can find of you are the wrappings and the trappings of how you might have been. Yet we have seen! We have seen your resurrection energy in a teenager paralyzed in a car accident who perseveres her way back to mobility. We have seen your resurrection strength in the companion who stays by our side through our darkest hours and carries the hope for us when our own resources fail. We have seen your resurrection joy in a child's delight over the first bluebells of spring. We have seen your resurrection hope in the amazing ability of our earth to regenerate life year after year in spite of our negligence. Lord, we see and we believe! May we ourselves become the carriers of your resurrection light into our world's darkness.

Acts 10:34, 37–43
Psalm 118
Colossians 3:1–4 or 1 Corinthians 5:6–8
John 20:1–9 or Matthew 28:1–10 or, at an afternoon or evening Mass, Luke 24:13–35

I saw the Lord ever before me,
with him at my right hand I shall not be disturbed.
Therefore my heart has been glad and my tongue has
exulted.

— ACTS 2:25 – 26

However deeply I delve into the story of my life,
I can find no situation that hasn't been prefigured
by the story of your living and dying. It helps
me find meaning in my chaos; it brings calm to
my storms and joy to my journeying.

Acts 2:14, 22–33
Psalm 16
Matthew 28:8–15

*But Mary stayed outside the tomb weeping. . . . Jesus said
to her, "Woman, why are you weeping? Whom are you
looking for?" She thought it was the gardener and said to
him, "Sir, if you carried him away, tell me where you laid
him, and I will take him." Jesus said to her, "Mary!" She
turned and said to him in Hebrew, "Rabbouni," which
means Teacher.*

— JOHN 20:11, 15 – 16

When tears blind our eyes and sadness prevents
us from hearing, we often draw the curtains on
our lives, and we miss the daybreak when it
dawns. At times like that, only your touch can
tear down the veil that comes between us.

Acts 2:36–41
Psalm 33
John 20:11–18

*Peter said [to the crippled beggar at the temple gate],
"I have neither silver nor gold, but what I do have I give
you: in the name of Jesus Christ the Nazorean, [rise and]
walk."*

— ACTS 3:6

The two friends rarely exchanged material gifts.
There was no need to. Instead, they exchanged
an unselfish, unconditional love, through which
each empowered the other to become his true
self, fully alive.

Acts 3:1–10
Psalm 105
Luke 24:13–35

Thursday

APRIL 4

While they were still speaking about this, he stood in their midst and said to them, "Peace be with you." But they were startled and terrified and thought that they were seeing a ghost. Then he said to them, "Why are you troubled? And why do questions arise in your hearts? Look at my hands and my feet, that it is I myself. Touch me and see, because a ghost does not have flesh and bones as you can see I have." And as he said this, he showed them his hands and his feet. . . . [T]hey were still incredulous for joy and were amazed.

— LUKE 24:36 – 41

And today, no less than when you lived and died on earth,
your Spirit dwells in the solid flesh and bones of our bodies,
and you show us your wounds when you show us those of
our sisters and brothers.

Acts 3:11–26
Psalm 8
Luke 24:35–48

Friday

APRIL 5

• SAINT VINCENT FERRER, PRIEST •

*When it was already dawn, Jesus was standing on the
shore; but the disciples did not realize that it was Jesus.
Jesus said to them, "Children, have you caught anything
to eat?" They answered him, "No." So he said to them,
"Cast the net over the right side of the boat and you will
find something." So they cast it, and were not able to pull it
in because of the number of fish.*

— JOHN 21:4 – 6

We stubbornly go on dredging the depths of our
own spent resources in search of a meager meal
while you wait for us to turn around and
recognize the feast you have prepared for us.

Acts 4:1–12
Psalm 118
John 21:1–14

*He said to them, "Go into the whole world and proclaim the
gospel to every creature."*

— MARK 16:15

When every creature breathes unpolluted air and
every fish swims in uncontaminated water, we
too shall be whole: creatures and creator,
eternally reconnected.

Acts 4:13–21
Psalm 118
Mark 16:9–15

Sunday

APRIL 7

• DAYLIGHT SAVING TIME BEGINS •

This is the day the LORD has made;
let us rejoice in it and be glad.

— PSALM 118:24

It was the worst day Jim had ever experienced.
Every hour had pitched him deeper into despair.
Nothing and nobody seemed to be on his side.
At bedtime his little daughter came to say good-
night, her eyes sad and uncomprehending.
Something in her gaze opened the floodgates of
his grief. The tears rose. He held the child close.
She had torn aside the veil of darkness, and he
had caught a glimpse of starlight. It had become,
after all, a day with a crack in it through which
God's love might find entrance.

Acts 2:42–47
Psalm 118
1 Peter 1:3–9
John 20:19–31

Behold, I am the handmaid of the Lord. May it be done to me according to your word.

— LUKE 1:38

Our response to the call of your love is made not only for ourselves but for all creation. It matters how we choose. Our yes counts.

Isaiah 7:10–14; 8:10
Psalm 30
Hebrews 10:4–10
Luke 1:26–38

Tuesday
APRIL 9

*The wind blows where it wills, and you can hear the sound
it makes, but you do not know where it comes from or where
it goes; so it is with everyone who is born of the Spirit.*

— JOHN 3:8

We think we know, yet we know not, where we
came from and where we are going. We only
know that we are making the journey with you,
and like the migrating geese, we must trust the
inner compass you have placed in our hearts.

Acts 4:32–37
Psalm 93
John 3:7–15

⇒ 132 ⇐

For everyone who does wicked things hates the light and does not come toward the light, so that his works might not be exposed. But whoever lives the truth comes to the light, so that his works may be clearly seen as done in God.

— JOHN 3:20 – 21

When we find the courage to come out of the darkness and face the truth about who we really are, we discover an unexpected bonus: the light also reveals to us the hurts and needs of our sisters and brothers.

Acts 5:17–26
Psalm 34
John 3:16–21

The one who is of the earth is earthly and speaks of earthly
things. But the one who comes from heaven [is above all].
He testifies to what he has seen and heard.

— JOHN 3 : 31 – 32

I come to you in prayer with mud on my feet,
bringing my earthly self with my earthbound
hopes and needs. You send me back to earth
with a grain of heaven in my heart, to be sown
back into the earth of my today.

Acts 5:27–33
Psalm 34
John 3:31–36

Friday

APRIL 12

*When Jesus raised his eyes and saw that a large crowd
was coming to him, he said to Philip, "Where can we buy
enough food for them to eat?" . . . Philip answered him,
"Two hundred days' wages worth of food would not be
enough for each of them to have a little [bit]." One of his
disciples, Andrew, the brother of Simon Peter, said to him,
"There is a boy here who has five barley loaves and two
fish; but what good are these for so many?"*

— JOHN 6:5, 7–9

Our much provides almost nothing. Your almost
nothing provides a feast.

Acts 5:34–42
Psalm 27
John 6:1–15

It had already grown dark, and Jesus had not yet come to them. The sea was stirred up because a strong wind was blowing. When they had rowed about three or four miles, they saw Jesus walking on the sea and coming near the boat, and they began to be afraid. But he said to them, "It is I. Do not be afraid." They wanted to take him into the boat, but the boat immediately arrived at the shore to which they were heading.

— JOHN 6:17–21

In our need, we are so concerned with bringing you on board our little boat that we forget that you hold all the power of the oceans in your hands.

Acts 6:1–7
Psalm 33
John 6:16–21

*And it happened that, while he was with them at table, he
took bread, said the blessing, broke it, and gave it to them.
With that their eyes were opened and they recognized him,
but he vanished from their sight. Then they said to each
other, "Were not our hearts burning [within us] while he
spoke to us on the way and opened the scriptures to us?"*

— LUKE 24:30 – 32

Amid all our blind wandering and searching,
there are moments of vision and clarity when we
know that we have met you along the roads of
our lives. The flame that you kindle in our hearts
in such moments becomes the beacon that leads
us onward.

Acts 2:14, 22–33
Psalm 16
1 Peter 1:17–21
Luke 24:13–35

Do not work for food that perishes but for the food that endures for eternal life.

— JOHN 6:27

I stopped beside a colleague's desk and noticed the photographs of his two children propped up proudly against his files. "That's to remind me why I'm really here," he told me. "When I'm tempted to pack it all in, I look at them and I know I'm working for something much more precious than a salary." And I knew that my colleague was working for hope, working for love.

Acts 6:8–15
Psalm 119
John 6:22–29

APRIL 16

So [the Jews] said to him, "What sign can you do, that we may see and believe in you? What can you do? Our ancestors ate manna in the desert."

— JOHN 6:30 – 31

"Prove that you love me," he said to her. "Do what I want." It was the end of their friendship. She found someone to whom she could give her love, someone who did not demand it.

Acts 7:51–8:1
Psalm 31
John 6:30–35

I came down from heaven not to do my own will but the will of the one who sent me.

— JOHN 6:38

In the still, silent center of prayer we are touched by the power of your will, your desire for our wholeness. Then we are sent to the outer edges of our lives and our world to carry out your desire, from the darkness of prayer to the light of action.

Acts 8:1–8
Psalm 66
John 6:35–40

≥ 140 ≤

*No one can come to me unless the Father who sent me
draw him.*

— JOHN 6:44

Jake tipped the iron filings out of the container
and onto the sheet of paper, as the science
teacher had told him to do. The filings lay there,
quite lifeless and pointless. Then he held the
magnet beneath the paper and gently moved it
around, watching as the filings moved toward the
power that was so much greater than they were,
as they followed the deepest laws of their nature.

Acts 8:26–40
Psalm 66
John 6:44–51

On his journey, as [Saul] was nearing Damascus, a light from the sky suddenly flashed around him. He fell to the ground and heard a voice saying to him, "Saul, Saul, why are you persecuting me?"

— ACTS 9:3 – 4

Gemma's nerves had been stretched to their breaking point, yet she knew there was no excuse for the way she had turned on her little son and made him the focus of all her frustration. It was nearly midnight when she started down the hall to bed, still seething with resentment. As she passed the nursery, something drew her in. The night-light was still burning. Its glow fell like a ray from heaven across the child's tearstained face. "Gemma," she seemed to hear her heart reproach her, "why are you being so untrue to yourself?"

Acts 9:1–20
Psalm 117
John 6:52–59

As a result of this, many [of] his disciples returned to their former way of life and no longer accompanied him. Jesus then said to the Twelve, "Do you also want to leave?" Simon Peter answered him, "Master, to whom shall we go? You have the words of eternal life. We have come to believe and are convinced that you are the Holy One of God."

— JOHN 6:66–69

Once we have met ourselves in you and have been stripped of all our masks and defenses, there can be no turning back. To turn away again would be to violate the very heart of our own reality.

Acts 9:31–42
Psalm 116
John 6:60–69

I came so that they might have life and have it more abundantly.

— JOHN 10:10

Twenty years ago the doctors had advised a termination. Jean and Gary gripped each other's hands as they remembered how their damaged little daughter had grown to her fullness. That growth had come out of heartbreakingly hard work, but it had made her feel complete, and for them, it was beyond anything they could have imagined.

Acts 2:14, 36–41
Psalm 23
1 Peter 2:20–25
John 10:1–10

My being thirsts for God, the living God.
When can I go and see the face of God?
— PSALM 42:3

The whole being of the crocus was concentrated
on its thirst for the water that nourished its
hidden secret. All through the winter it pushed
determinedly, blindly, toward its still unknown
fulfillment, until on a cold March morning, it
opened its flower to the full glory of the
springtime sunshine.

Acts 11:1–18
Psalm 42
John 10:11–18

• SAINT GEORGE, MARTYR • SAINT ADALBERT, BISHOP AND MARTYR •

Within you is my true home.

— PSALM 87:7

There were some unlikely bedfellows in the
animal rescue center. In the wild they would have
been implacable enemies or predators upon one
other. But in their pain and their helplessness they
lay side by side, drawn together by the loving
hands that ministered to them.

Acts 11:19–26
Psalm 87
John 10:22–30

May God be gracious to us and bless us;
may God's face shine upon us.
So shall your rule be known upon the earth,
your saving power among all the nations.

— PSALM 67:2 – 3

Let your light shine upon us, Lord, so that we
may reflect that light for others, as cats' eyes
reflect light to help other night travelers find
their way.

Acts 12:24–13:5
Psalm 67
John 12:44–50

Thursday

APRIL 25

*[Jesus] said to them, "Go into the whole world and
proclaim the gospel to every creature."*

— MARK 16:15

You come to us in the intimate moments of our
everyday lives, and then you send us out to the
farthest reaches of creation, like ripples on a
lake, giving us to carry the healing touch of your
love and your peace.

1 Peter 5:5–14
Psalm 89
Mark 16:15–20

Do not let your hearts be troubled. You have faith in God;
have faith also in me.

— JOHN 14:1

Alison climbed the mountain with labored steps
and painful breaths. She knew that at the end of
all the climbing she would be standing on the
roof of the world and viewing the full glory of
the mountains. Her trust in that vision made
every hardship worthwhile.

Acts 13:26–33
Psalm 2
John 14:1–6

I have made you a light to the Gentiles, that you may be
an instrument of salvation to the ends of the earth.

— ACTS 13:47

When I blow out my prayer candle, the wisps of
smoke float off into every remote corner of the
house. That is when prayer really begins—when
the light goes out into the dark places.

Acts 13:44–52
Psalm 98
John 14:7–14

Behold, I am laying a stone in Zion,
a cornerstone, chosen and precious,
and whoever believes in it shall not be put to shame.

—1 PETER 2:6

You resisted the temptation to leap in glory from the pinnacle of the temple; instead you consented to become its living foundation stone, to be either carelessly walked over or trustfully built upon.

Acts 6:1–7
Psalm 33
1 Peter 2:4–9
John 14:1–12

May you be blessed by the LORD,
who made heaven and earth.
The heavens belong to the LORD,
but the earth is given to us.

— PSALM 115:15–16

We feel pangs of hurt and sadness when we realize that a gift we have given in love has been neglected, or used carelessly, or even willfully damaged. How do you feel, Lord, when you see how we treat your gift to us—this earth, our home?

Acts 14:5–18
Psalm 115
John 14:21–26

Peace I leave with you; my peace I give to you. Not as the world gives do I give it to you. Do not let your hearts be troubled or afraid.

— JOHN 14:27

As long as I stay in the battle zone of my own conflicting wants and fears, there is constant warfare in my heart. But when you draw me down into the deepest longing of my being, the tumult ceases, there is no more competition, and my heart feels whole again.

Acts 14:19–28
Psalm 145
John 14:27–31

⇒ 153 ⇐

Wednesday

MAY 1

• SAINT JOSEPH THE WORKER •

*I am the vine, you are the branches. Whoever remains in
me and I in him will bear much fruit, because without me
you can do nothing.*

— JOHN 15:5

When we have all gained our personal
independence and have established our own
little kingdoms, we will have finally completed
the fragmentation of your creation and the
destruction of ourselves and of each other.

Acts 15:1–6
Psalm 122
John 15:1–8 or (for memorial) Genesis 1:26–2:3 or Colossians 3:14–15, 17, 23–24
Matthew 13:54–58

Remain in my love. If you keep my commandments, you will remain in my love, just as I have kept my Father's commandments and remain in his love. I have told you this so that my joy might be in you and your joy might be complete.

— JOHN 15:9–11

Yet there is another way. We can reverse the process of destructive fragmentation; we do so every time we reach out to each other in love and every time we reach out to you in prayer. It is then that our longing for independence is replaced by a longing for wholeness.

Acts 15:7–21
Psalm 96
John 15:9–11

Friday

MAY 3

• SAINTS PHILIP AND JAMES, APOSTLES •

*Philip said to him, "Master, show us the Father, and that
will be enough for us." Jesus said to him, "Have I been with
you for so long a time and you still do not know me,
Philip? Whoever has seen me has seen the Father."*

— JOHN 14:8 – 9

When I hold an acorn in my hand, I hold the
encoded reality of the full-grown oak. So you
too, Lord, carry the fullness of the Father in your
human life, and you call us, your brothers and
sisters, to carry his fullness in our lives.

1 Corinthians 15:1–8
Psalm 19
John 14:6–14

If you belonged to the world, the world would love its own;
but because you do not belong to the world, and I have
chosen you out of the world, the world hates you.

— JOHN 15:19

Oscar Romero was shot to the ground in the
very act of celebrating Mass, fearlessly
proclaiming your love with his last breath. The
greater the power of the light, the more
intensely it will provoke the power of darkness,
until all darkness is dispelled and only the Light
remains, eternally.

Acts 16:1–10
Psalm 100
John 15:18–21

I will not leave you orphans. . . .
On that day you will realize that I am in my Father and
you are in me and I in you.
— JOHN 14:18, 20

In the here and now we may feel far apart from
each other and very alone, but in the eternal
reality of All-that-Is, we are one with each other
and one in you.

Acts 8:5–8, 14–17
Psalm 66
1 Peter 3:15–18
John 14:15–21

*They will expel you from the synagogues; in fact, the hour
is coming when everyone who kills you will think he is
offering worship to God. They will do this because they
have not known either the Father or me.*

— JOHN 16:2 – 3

The gulf between Barbara and her son widened
daily as their quarrel over his girlfriend
deepened. Barbara refused to have the girl in the
house or to hear anything good about her. "If
you knew her, you wouldn't react like this," he
protested. But Barbara didn't want to know.

Acts 16:11–15
Psalm 149
John 15:26–16:4

About midnight, while Paul and Silas were praying and singing hymns to God as the prisoners listened, there was suddenly such a severe earthquake that the foundations of the jail shook; all the doors flew open, and the chains of all were pulled loose.

— ACTS 16:25 – 26

The earthshaking force of our lives' worst experiences can bring about a radical remaking, preparing us for our lives' most powerful growth and opening up the doors of our hearts to your redeeming liberation.

Acts 16:22–34
Psalm 138
John 16:5–11

I have much more to tell you, but you cannot bear it now.
But when he comes, the Spirit of truth, he will guide you to
all truth.

— JOHN 16:12 – 13

We stop short of the truth for many reasons:
out of fear of what it might reveal and of the
consequences to ourselves, out of the love that
seeks to shelter others from pain. Before we can
face the completeness of your truth, we need
you to free us fully from our fears and to open us
fully to your healing love.

Acts 17:15, 22–18:1
Psalm 148
John 16:12–15

Thursday

MAY 9

• THE ASCENSION OF THE LORD •

And behold, I am with you always, until the end of the age.

— MATTHEW 28:20

With us always—even when we are walking
away from you, especially when we are sure we
can manage without you, and precisely when we
feel you have given up on us. . . . With us
always and closer to us than we are to ourselves.

Acts 1:1–11
Psalm 47
Ephesians 1:17–23
Matthew 28:16–20

*So you also are now in anguish. But I will see you again,
and your hearts will rejoice, and no one will take your joy
away from you.*

— JOHN 16:22

We may gather the fruit of happiness painlessly,
as we do blackberries at the roadside which are
easily reached. But joy is a more elusive fruit,
and it often lies beyond a barrier of thorns, on
the other side of sorrow.

Acts 18:9–18
Psalm 47
John 16:20–23

Ask and you will receive, so that your joy may be complete.

— JOHN 16:24

When we reveal our needs to you, we are bringing
you the empty spaces of our hearts so you can fill
them. Unless we open our empty hands, how can
you fill them with our daily bread?

Acts 18:23–28
Psalm 47
John 16:23–28

Sunday

MAY 12

• MOTHER'S DAY •

When they entered the city they went to the upper room
where they were staying. . . . All these devoted themselves
with one accord to prayer, together with some women, and
Mary the mother of Jesus, and his brothers.

— ACTS 1:13 –14

And still, as the earth spins from dawn to dusk,
from east to west, the never-ceasing prayer of
those who seek you forms an unbroken chain of
faith that encircles all of creation with your love.

Acts 1:12–14
Psalm 27
1 Peter 4:13–16
John 17:1–11

⋙ 165 ⋘

I have told you this so that you might have peace in me. In the world you will have trouble, but take courage, I have conquered the world.

— JOHN 16:33

Armchair believing may provide a comfortable sanctuary amid life's storms, but our faith becomes authentic when it is sharpened on the cutting edge of challenge, struggle, and opposition.

Acts 19:1–8
Psalm 68
John 16:29–33

*It was not you who chose me, but I who chose you and
appointed you to go and bear fruit that will remain, so that
whatever you ask the Father in my name he may give you.
This I command you: love one another.*

— JOHN 15:16–17

Everything comes from you, Lord. You choose.
You send us out. You make us fruitful. All you ask
of us is that we respond to all with love.

Acts 1:15–17, 20–26
Psalm 113
John 15:9–17

*I do not ask that you take them out of the world but that
you keep them from the evil one.*

— JOHN 17:15

When the storms blow against me, my
instinctive prayer is to ask you to transplant me
to a safer, more welcoming place. You answer my
prayer by leaving me where I am, in the eye of
the storm, where I find my true center in you.

Acts 20:28–38
Psalm 68
John 17:11–19

*I pray not only for them, but also for those who will believe
in me through their word, so that they may all be one.*

— JOHN 17:20 – 21

Two thousand years ago you stood among your
first disciples and prayed for us. Today your
Spirit lives in our hearts and echoes that prayer
back to you, its source.

Acts 22:30; 23:6–11
Psalm 16
John 17:20–26

He said to him the third time, "Simon, son of John, do you
love me?" Peter . . . said to him, "Lord, you know
everything; you know that I love you." [Jesus] said to him,
"Feed my sheep."

— JOHN 21:17

The measure of our loving is always in the
warmth of our giving.

Acts 25:13–21
Psalm 103
John 21:15–19

There are also many other things that Jesus did, but if these were to be described individually, I do not think the whole world would contain the books that would be written.

— JOHN 21:25

Your gospel is written indelibly, uniquely, on every believer's heart, and all creation is too small to contain its living presence.

Acts 28:16–20, 30–31
Psalm 11
John 21:20–25

Sunday

MAY 19

• PENTECOST SUNDAY •

*Then there appeared to them tongues as of fire, which parted and came to
rest on each one of them. And they were all filled with the holy Spirit
and began to speak in different tongues, as the Spirit enabled them to
proclaim.*

— ACTS 2:3 – 4

The flame of your Spirit is divided to dwell in each
believing heart, but in its division it is not diminished but
multiplied so that the whole of your creation might catch
your light and your fire.

VIGIL:
Genesis 11:1–9 or Exodus 19:3–8, 16–20 or Ezekiel 37:1–14 or Joel 3:1–5
Psalm 104
Romans 8:22–27
John 7:37–39

DAY:
Acts 2:1–11
Psalm 104
1 Corinthians 12:3–7, 12–13
John 20:19–23

"If you can do anything, have compassion on us and help us." Jesus said to him, " 'If you can?' Everything is possible to one who has faith." Then the boy's father cried out, "I do believe, help my unbelief!"

— MARK 9:22 – 24

Out of our darkness we cry, "Help the little faith we have!" And that turns out to be the most potent prayer of all. It opens us up to your healing and makes all things possible.

James 3:13–18
Psalm 19
Mark 9:14–29

*Where do the wars and where do the conflicts among you
come from? Is it not from your passions that make war
within your members? You covet but do not possess. You
kill and envy but you cannot obtain; you fight and wage
war. You do not possess because you do not ask.*

— JAMES 4:1– 2

I turned on the news and saw my own inner
conflicts revealed. I saw the inner struggles of
every member of the human family stamped
onto a barren battlefield and scarred indelibly
across the faces of the innocent. Then I turned
off the television and knew that peace could
begin only with me.

James 4:1–10
Psalm 55
Mark 9:30–37

You have no idea what your life will be like tomorrow. You are a puff of smoke that appears briefly and then disappears.

— JAMES 4:14

A mist can obscure the beauty of life from ourselves and from others. Or it can soak into the earth and give life to new growth. Which will our lives become: an obscuring cloud or a refreshing dewfall?

James 4:13–17
Psalm 49
Mark 9:38–40

≥ 175 ≤

Salt is good, but if salt becomes insipid, with what will you restore its flavor? Keep salt in yourselves and you will have peace with one another.

— MARK 9:50

May the salt of our faith be the salt that preserves and the salt that gives flavor, the salt that melts frozen hearts and the salt that tempts the seeker to taste and see. May the salt of our faith become salt for the earth.

James 5:1–6
Psalm 49
Mark 9:41–50

Let your "Yes" mean "Yes" and your "No" mean "No."
— JAMES 5:12

The hallmark of truth is its simplicity.
Complications and convolutions are the
symptoms of concealment. Simplicity is of God.
The complications are our own.

James 5:9–12
Psalm 103
Mark 10:1–12

My brothers, if anyone among you should stray from the truth and someone bring him back, he should know that whoever brings back a sinner from the error of his way will save his soul from death and will cover a multitude of sins.

— JAMES 5:19 – 20

One return to the way of truth is worth a hundred reproaches for deviating from it.

James 5:13–20
Psalm 141
Mark 10:13–16

*Agree with one another, live in peace, and the God of love
and peace will be with you.*

— 2 CORINTHIANS 13:11

The peace of "shalom" restores us to wholeness,
within ourselves and with all creation. To know
"shalom," to share "shalom," is to be at home
with God.

Exodus 34:4–6, 8–9
Daniel 3:52–56
2 Corinthians 13:11–13
John 3:16–18

Blessed be the God and Father of our Lord Jesus Christ, who in his great mercy gave us a new birth to . . . a salvation that is ready to be revealed in the final time. In this you rejoice, although now for a little while you may have to suffer through various trials, so that the genuineness of your faith, more precious than gold that is perishable even though tested by fire, may prove to be for praise, glory, and honor at the revelation of Jesus Christ.

—1 PETER 1:3, 5–7

In the crucible of your redeeming grace, it sometimes feels as though our faith, our hope, and everything we think we are is consumed to ashes. Yet those ashes are Gethsemane ashes, and from them alone will the fullness of your resurrection arise.

1 Peter 1:3–9
Psalm 111
Mark 10:17–27

Many that are first will be last, and [the] last will be first.
— MARK 10:31

The prayer group gathered as usual for reflection
and faith sharing. They had been praying
together for several years and felt confident and
experienced. Sally had never attended the
gathering before and hardly knew how to begin.
But as soon as she shared, quietly and shyly, the
joy she felt when she met with you in prayer, they
knew they were in the presence of one who knew
you in her heart and carried that knowledge
unconsciously to everyone around her.

1 Peter 1:10–16
Psalm 98
Mark 10:28–31

Conduct yourselves with reverence during the time of your sojourning, realizing that you were ransomed from your futile conduct, handed on by your ancestors, not with perishable things like silver or gold but with the precious blood of Christ as of a spotless unblemished lamb.

—1 PETER 1:17–19

The checkout girl took my twenty-dollar bill and routinely examined it for signs of counterfeiting before completing the transaction. I packed my groceries, reflecting that this bag of perishable food had been purchased with corruptible currency, while remembering that what is indestructible in me has been purchased by your incorruptible love.

1 Peter 1:18–25
Psalm 147
Mark 10:32–45

[Bartimaeus] threw aside his cloak, sprang up, and came to Jesus. Jesus said to him in reply, "What do you want me to do for you?" The blind man replied to him, "Master, I want to see."

— MARK 10:50 – 51

The heart of our own deepest desires and longings is where we will meet your dream for us and realize the certainty of its fulfillment.

1 Peter 2:2–5, 9–12
Psalm 100
Mark 10:46–52

⋟ 183 ⋞

Friday

MAY 31

When Elizabeth heard Mary's greeting, the infant leaped in her womb, and Elizabeth, filled with the holy Spirit, cried out in a loud voice and said, "Most blessed are you among women, and blessed is the fruit of your womb."

— LUKE 1:41–42

When heart speaks to heart, the yet-unborn Christ in me leaps in recognition of the yet-unborn Christ in you.

Zephaniah 3:14–18 or Romans 12:9–16
Isaiah 12:2–6
Luke 1:39–56

≥ 184 ≤

*Keep yourselves in the love of God and wait for the mercy
of our Lord Jesus Christ that leads to eternal life.*

— JUDE 21

After the shooting, the dazed survivors of the
shattered community crept helplessly into the
church to huddle together in their grief, in their
need of each other, and in their overwhelming
need of you.

Jude 17–25
Psalm 63
Mark 11:27–33

⇒ 185 ⇐

The cup of blessing that we bless, is it not a participation
in the blood of Christ? The bread that we break, is it not a
participation in the body of Christ?

—1 CORINTHIANS 10:16

Colin had made great plans for the day, and he
knew what he wanted to accomplish. But when
evening came, he looked back over a whole
series of interruptions. He had broken off one
piece of the day after another, giving his time
and loving attention to those who had asked for
it. He had broken his day into living pieces of
himself and had shared it with others. He had
celebrated a living communion with you.

Deuteronomy 8:2–3, 14–16
Psalm 147
1 Corinthians 10:16–17
John 6:51–58

His divine power has bestowed on us everything that makes for life and devotion, through the knowledge of him who called us by his own glory and power. Through these, he has bestowed on us the precious and very great promises.

— 2 PETER 1:3 – 4

In every lived moment we discover your gifts, and every gift is a sacrament, at once both fulfilling the needs of the "now" and pointing to, and bringing to fulfillment, the promise of the "not yet."

2 Peter 1:2–7
Psalm 91
Mark 12:1–12

Tuesday

JUNE 4

Show your deeds to your servants,
your glory to their children.
— PSALM 90:16

The brilliance of the full moon held me rooted
to the spot in awe and wonder. Yet it was only a
lump of rock spinning through space, and its
glory came entirely from the light of the unseen
sun, which was shining upon it in the darkness
of my night. It shed upon me its promise that we
too, your lumps of clay, might reflect the light of
your unseen presence into the darkness we find
around us.

2 Peter 3:12–15, 17–18
Psalm 90
Mark 12:13–17

He is not God of the dead but of the living.

— MARK 12:27

When I dwell on the follies and the failures of my past, I find nothing but an empty tomb. But when I hear you call my name in the garden of my grief, I know that you are touching that which is alive in me and are calling it into resurrection.

2 Timothy 1:1–3, 6–12
Psalm 123
Mark 12:18–27

Thursday

JUNE 6

• SAINT NORBERT, BISHOP •

If we deny him
he will deny us.
If we are unfaithful
he remains faithful,
for he cannot deny himself.

— 2 TIMOTHY 2:12 –13

We can disown only what is not part of us.
When God has made his dwelling in our hearts,
faithfulness must follow.

2 Timothy 2:8–15
Psalm 25
Mark 12:28–34

⇒ 190 ⇐

Come to me, all you who labor and are burdened, and I will give you rest. Take my yoke upon you and learn from me, for I am meek and humble of heart; and you will find rest for yourselves. For my yoke is easy, and my burden light.

— MATTHEW 11:28 – 30

The work is easy when the yoke fits the ox for which it is designed. Our work runs smoothly when we are engaged in what you most want us to do.

Deuteronomy 7:6–11
Psalm 103
1 John 4:7–16
Matthew 11:25–30

Saturday

JUNE 8

• THE IMMACULATE HEART OF MARY •

For I am already being poured out like a libation, and the time of my departure is at hand.

— 2 TIMOTHY 4:6

The power of your Spirit in our hearts is released only when we accept the risk of our own emptiness and allow you to pour us out for others.

2 Timothy 4:1–8
Psalm 71
Luke 2:41–51

⇒ 192 ⇐

He will come to us like the rain,
like spring rain that waters the earth.

— HOSEA 6:3

Amid the clamor of my spoken prayers and
pleadings, Lord, how easily I forget that underneath
it all you are constantly nourishing those longings
that my heart and words cannot express.

Hosea 6:3–6
Psalm 50
Romans 4:18–25
Matthew 9:9–13

Monday

J U N E 10

*Blessed are you when they insult you and persecute you and
utter every kind of evil against you [falsely] because of me.
Rejoice and be glad, for your reward will be great in heaven.*

— MATTHEW 5:11–12

Etty went to her death in a concentration camp
with her eyes open: not condoning or cooperating
with the evil, but knowing that the inner source of
the joy in her heart was more powerful still.
Knowing you, and blessed in that knowledge
whose roots are deeper than all destruction.

1 Kings 17:1–6
Psalm 121
Matthew 5:1–12

Tuesday

JUNE 11

*But you have given my heart more joy than they have
when grain and wine abound.*

— PSALM 4:8

We rejoice briefly in the harvest suppers of our
lives, but the joy you give us will sustain us
through all our wintering.

Acts 11:21–26; 13:1–3
Psalm 4
Matthew 5:13–16

⊰ 195 ⊱

Answer me, LORD! Answer me, that this people may know that you, LORD, are God and that you have brought them back to their senses.

—1 KINGS 18:37

When our own lives reveal the radiance of our joy in you, we cooperate in your winning back of the hearts of all creation.

1 Kings 18:20–39
Psalm 16
Matthew 5:17–19

• SAINT ANTHONY OF PADUA, PRIEST AND DOCTOR OF THE CHURCH •

Thus do you prepare the earth:
you drench plowed furrows,
and level their ridges.
With showers you keep the ground soft,
blessing its young sprouts.

— PSALM 65:10–11

Sometimes our lives fill up with sorrow and the
sharp blades of pain drive furrows through our
hearts. Saturate us, then, with your grace so that
we might know that in just such times you are
blessing and nourishing our growth.

1 Kings 18:41–46
Psalm 65
Matthew 5:20–26

⋛ 197 ⋚

Friday

JUNE 14

And if your right hand causes you to sin, cut it off and throw it away. It is better for you to lose one of your members than to have your whole body go into Gehenna.
— MATTHEW 5:30

When I look around the inner rooms of my heart I find gifts from you that I have allowed to become the center of my life. Help me to give them back to you, Lord, and to build my life on the giver, not the gifts.

1 Kings 19:9, 11–16
Psalm 27
Matthew 5:27–32

Let your "Yes" mean "Yes," and your "No" mean "No."
Anything more is from the evil one.

— MATTHEW 5:37

Mary eventually put down the letter in irritation,
annoyed by all its expressions of "You really
shouldn't have gone to all that trouble" and
"How can we ever repay you for your kindness?"
They didn't quite ring true. It was so refreshing
to read the simple response of her friend: "Thank
you for the evening. I loved it."

1 Kings 19:19–21
Psalm 16
Matthew 5:33–37

Cure the sick, raise the dead, cleanse lepers, drive out demons. Without cost you have received; without cost you are to give.

— MATTHEW 10:8

A gentle touch on a feverish forehead. A warm greeting to revive hope in dead spirits. An embrace of acceptance. A word of affirmation. All freely given and asking nothing more of us but that we freely pass them on.

Exodus 19:2–6
Psalm 100
Romans 5:6–11
Matthew 9:36–10:8

Give to the one who asks of you, and do not turn your back on one who wants to borrow.

— MATTHEW 5:42

Peter was getting tired of opening the rectory door to beggars and vagrants. Enough was enough. Then Charlie knocked and Peter looked into his eyes and gave again. A tear of gratitude trickled down Charlie's cheek. There will never be enough giving until all is spent.

1 Kings 21:1–16
Psalm 5
Matthew 5:38–42

Have mercy on me, God, in your goodness;
in your abundant compassion blot out my offense.
Wash away all my guilt;
from my sin cleanse me.

— PSALM 51:3 – 4

The pickax of reproach may hack at our stony
hearts, but only the ceaseless, gentle, cleansing
flow of grace will soften them into flesh.

1 Kings 21:17–29
Psalm 51
Matthew 5:43–48

But when you give alms, do not let your left hand know what your right is doing, so that your almsgiving may be secret. And your Father who sees in secret will repay you.

— MATTHEW 6 : 3 – 4

Everyone in the neighborhood knew of Eileen's legendary generosity. Everyone, that is, except Eileen herself, who never gave it a thought as she lived out her life in unself-conscious attentiveness to the needs of those around her.

2 Kings 2:1, 6–14
Psalm 31
Matthew 6:1–6, 16–18

≥ 203 ≤

The LORD is king; let the earth rejoice;
let the many islands be glad.
Cloud and darkness surround the Lord;
justice and right are the foundation of his throne.

— PSALM 97:1–2

Why, Lord, do you walk the earth in the shape
of those who are clouded with despair and
darkened by suffering? Is it to awaken in us the
desire to bring them your justice and your
healing love?

Sirach 48:1–14
Psalm 97
Matthew 6:7–15

Friday

JUNE 21

• SAINT ALOYSIUS GONZAGA, RELIGIOUS •

For where your treasure is, there also will your heart be.

— MATTHEW 6:21

It began harmlessly for Jim. First it was a few hours of overtime for an extra holiday, then it was a few more for a bigger house, and finally he was leading a compulsive, workaholic lifestyle that left his heart stranded on the beach of his ebbing life.

2 Kings 11:1–4, 9–18, 20
Psalm 132
Matthew 6:19–23

I will punish their crime with a rod
and their guilt with lashes.
But I will not take my love from him,
nor will I betray my bond of loyalty.

— PSALM 89:33 – 34

It had been a terrible day, and Susan's composure was in
shreds. An unruly toddler, a disobedient child, and a moody
teenager had all taken their toll on their mother's nerves.
Finally, in the silence of the night, she slipped into their
rooms one last time. As she kissed them softly in their
sleep, her heart tugged itself back into place, and she knew,
once again, just how much she loved them.

2 Chronicles 24:17–25
Psalm 89
Matthew 6:24–34

Even all the hairs of your head are counted. So do not be afraid.

— MATTHEW 10:30 – 31

Joan held her newborn daughter in her arms, stroking each toe and each finger and caressing the tiny eyebrows with a love that would spend itself gladly in the years to come. Do you not hold us in tenderness too, Lord, and spend yourself in love for us? You, who are the source and wellspring of all our loving?

Jeremiah 20:10–13
Psalm 69
Romans 5:12–15
Matthew 10:26–33

And as John was completing his course, he would say, "What do you suppose that I am? I am not he. Behold, one is coming after me; I am not worthy to unfasten the sandals of his feet."

— ACTS 13:25

Give us the grace, Lord, to let our lives become pointers toward you and not destinations in themselves.

VIGIL:
Jeremiah 1:4–10
Psalm 71
1 Peter 1:8–12
Luke 1:5–17

DAY:
Isaiah 49:1–6
Psalm 139
Acts 13:22–26
Luke 1:57–66, 80

For out of Jerusalem shall come a remnant,
and from Mount Zion, survivors.
The zeal of the LORD of hosts shall do this.

— 2 KINGS 19:31

The seamless garment of your kingdom is not
made from the finest rolls of fabric, but from the
scraps and remnants of faith that you have
gathered from your people through the ages and
have made one in your love.

2 Kings 19:9–11, 14–21, 31–36
Psalm 48
Matthew 7:6, 12–14

Beware of false prophets, who come to you in sheep's clothing, but underneath are ravenous wolves. By their fruits you will know them. Do people pick grapes from thornbushes, or figs from thistles? Just so, every good tree bears good fruit, and a rotten tree bears bad fruit.

— MATTHEW 7:15 –17

The creatures of the woodland know how to distinguish between the colorful, seductive toadstools and the humble, nondescript mushrooms because they have noticed their effects. Lord, please give us the same wisdom to use in our lives and in our world.

2 Kings 22:8–13; 23:1–3
Psalm 119
Matthew 7:15–20

Everyone who listens to these words of mine and acts on them will be like a wise man who built his house on rock. The rain fell, the floods came, and the winds blew and buffeted the house. But it did not collapse; it had been set solidly on rock.

— MATTHEW 7:24 – 25

We place our trust in our home and in our job and in our investments, yet the storms of recession and war destroy them. And when all is gone, we are left with nothing but the hard rock and the shocked realization that only that rock will be able to hold us.

2 Kings 24:8–17
Psalm 79
Matthew 7:21–29

Friday

JUNE 28

• SAINT IRENAEUS, BISHOP AND MARTYR •

By the rivers of Babylon
we sat mourning and weeping
when we remembered Zion. . . .
But how could we sing a song of the LORD
in a foreign land?

— PSALM 137:1, 4

Yet when we find the heart to sing your song in a world that rejects you, our little patch of alien soil becomes your home again and a place where others might find you.

2 Kings 25:1–12
Psalm 137
Matthew 8:1–4

On the very night before Herod was to bring him to trial, Peter, secured by double chains, was sleeping between two soldiers, while outside the door guards kept watch on the prison. Suddenly the angel of the Lord stood by him and a light shone in the cell. He tapped Peter on the side and awakened him, saying, "Get up quickly." The chains fell from his wrists.

— ACTS 12:6–7

Break into the prison of our fears, Lord, and shine the light of your love. With your word, silence the cries of our anxiety. Turn our hearts to you so that the shadow of our fears falls behind us.

VIGIL:	*DAY:*
Acts 3:1–10	Acts 12:1–11
Psalm 19	Psalm 34
Galatians 1:11–20	2 Timothy 4:6–8, 17–18
John 21:15–19	Matthew 16:13–19

Whoever finds his life will lose it, and whoever loses his life for my sake will find it.

— MATTHEW 10:39

When I settle down, comfortable in my own certainties, I am sovereign of my own little domain, but if I embrace the challenge of acknowledging my uncertainties, the whole of creation is mine to discover and rejoice in.

2 Kings 4:8–11, 14–16
Psalm 89
Romans 6:3–4, 8–11
Matthew 10:37–42

A scribe approached and said to him, "Teacher, I will
follow you wherever you go." Jesus answered him, "Foxes
have dens and birds of the sky have nests, but the Son of
Man has nowhere to rest his head."

— MATTHEW 8:19 – 20

Everyone said that Mark had really "arrived." He
seemed to have achieved all his dreams, and his
lifestyle reflected his success. Then he met you
and became one of your people of the way, for
whom there is no arrival, except in you and in
your homeless journeying.

Amos 2:6–10, 13–16
Psalm 50
Matthew 8:18–22

Suddenly a violent storm came up on the sea, so that the boat was being swamped by waves; but he was asleep. They came and woke him, saying, "Lord, save us! We are perishing!"

— MATTHEW 8:24 – 25

Crying, Jennie went to her mother in the middle of the night to be comforted after waking from a nightmare. A more independent child—or one less loved—might have struggled on alone, suppressing the terror, and might never have known the calming reassurance of the loving presence of one who is always there for her.

Amos 3:1–8; 4:11–12
Psalm 5
Matthew 8:23–27

Then he said to Thomas, "Put your finger here and see my hands, and bring your hand and put it into my side, and do not be unbelieving, but believe." Thomas answered and said to him, "My Lord and my God!"

— JOHN 20:27–28

The reality of your living presence is something far beyond our imagination, Lord, but we begin to get in touch with it when we have the courage to touch the world's wounds with loving hearts and hands.

Ephesians 2:19–22
Psalm 117
John 20:24–29

Thursday

JULY 4

People brought to him a paralytic lying on a stretcher.
When Jesus saw their faith, he said to the paralytic,
"Courage, child, your sins are forgiven."

— MATTHEW 9:2

When we are paralyzed by the knowledge of our
own failures and fears, you free us by giving us
the courage to acknowledge our need and to let
you gently lift the crippling burdens of the past
from our hearts.

Amos 7:10–17
Psalm 19
Matthew 9:1–8

⇒ 218 ⇐

Yes, days are coming, says the Lord GOD,
when I will send famine upon the land:
Not a famine of bread, or thirst for water,
but for hearing the word of the LORD.
Then shall they wander from sea to sea
and rove from the north to the east
In search of the word of the LORD,
but they shall not find it.

— AMOS 8:11–12

Lord, we are one with your staggering,
wandering people, but we carry your living
water in our hearts to quench their parched
spirit because we are also one with you.

Amos 8:4–6, 9–12
Psalm 119
Matthew 9:9–13

No one patches an old cloak with a piece of unshrunken cloth, for its fullness pulls away from the cloak and the tear gets worse. People do not put new wine into old wineskins. Otherwise the skins burst, the wine spills out, and the skins are ruined. Rather, they pour new wine into fresh wineskins, and both are preserved.

— MATTHEW 9:16 –17

You do not call us to merely repair or make minor adjustments to our accustomed life in the world, but to make the radical transformation into a life lived in you.

Amos 9:11–15
Psalm 85
Matthew 9:14–17

JULY 7

Come to me, all you who labor and are burdened, and I will give you rest. Take my yoke upon you and learn from me, for I am meek and humble of heart; and you will find rest for yourselves. For my yoke is easy, and my burden light.

— MATTHEW 11:28–30

We find your promised rest not by evading the burdens of our lives but by carrying them on your strength. We find our deepest freedom when we are yoked to you.

Zechariah 9:9–10
Psalm 145
Romans 8:9, 11–13
Matthew 11:25–30

JULY 8

So I will allure her;
I will lead her into the desert
and speak to her heart.

— HOSEA 2:16

When we are walking through the desert spaces
in our lives and the searing sun is burning away
all our masks and defenses—there, where
nothing comes between you and us, we meet
you face to face, and you speak to our hearts.

Hosea 2:16–18, 21–22
Psalm 145
Matthew 9:18–26

⇒ 222 ⇐

At the sight of the crowds, his heart was moved with pity for them because they were troubled and abandoned, like sheep without a shepherd. Then he said to his disciples, "The harvest is abundant but the laborers are few; so ask the master of the harvest to send out laborers for his harvest."

— MATTHEW 9:36 – 38

The fields of my life are rich with the harvest of gifts you have planted uniquely in my heart. Yet if I fail to gather their fruits and share them with a hungry world, you will have planted them in vain.

Hosea 8:4–7, 11–13
Psalm 115
Matthew 9:32–38

Sow for yourselves justice,
reap the fruit of piety;
Break up for yourselves a new field,
for it is time to seek the LORD,
till he come and rain down justice upon you.

— HOSEA 10:12

Katy had lived a good and law-abiding life, yet when she looked back there seemed little to show for it. Then came the groundbreaking years, when unseen stirrings shook her life's soil apart. The waiting time had yielded to the coming of the harvest, and she knew that it was time to seek the Lord in the hidden roots of her being.

Hosea 10:1–3, 7–8, 12
Psalm 105
Matthew 10:1–7

Without cost you have received; without cost you are to give.

— MATTHEW 10:8

As long as we attach price tags and conditions to
our loving, we will not be fully free. And until
we are free we can never fully love.

Hosea 11:1–4, 8–9
Psalm 80
Matthew 10:7–15

I will heal their defection,
I will love them freely;
for my wrath is turned away from them.
I will be like the dew for Israel:
he shall blossom like the lily;
He shall strike root like the Lebanon cedar,
and put forth his shoots.

— HOSEA 14:5 –7

When the waves of anger and resentment
recede, I will see the firm sands and solid rock of
love. And there I will learn that I enslave and am
enslaved by what I resent, and I make fruitful
and am made fruitful by what I love.

Hosea 14:2–10
Psalm 51
Matthew 10:16–23

Then I heard the voice of the Lord saying, "Whom shall I send? Who will go for us?" "Here I am," I said; "send me!"
— ISAIAH 6:8

Barbara was terrified of driving, but when her neighbor had an accident she forgot her fear and drove him through rush-hour traffic to the hospital. There had been no time to spare for asking, "Who will drive?" There had only been time to make the instant response of love.

Isaiah 6:1–8
Psalm 93
Matthew 10:24–33

Thus do you prepare the earth:
you drench plowed furrows,
and level their ridges.
With showers you keep the ground soft,
blessing its young sprouts.

— PSALM 65:10 –11

The tears that flow through the dark and lonely
hours are the rains that soften our hearts, making
way for the compassion that can respond to the
darkness and the loneliness of others.

Isaiah 55:10–11
Psalm 65
Romans 8:18–23
Matthew 13:1–23 or 13:1–9

Do not think that I have come to bring peace upon the earth. I have come to bring not peace but the sword.

— MATTHEW 10:34

We do not reach your peace by staying out of trouble, but by painfully setting our course through all the struggles along our way and slicing through the obstructions that keep us from our truest destination.

Isaiah 1:10–17
Psalm 50
Matthew 10:34–11:1

───────────

≥ 229 ≤

Tuesday

JULY 16

Take care you remain tranquil and do not fear; let not your courage fail.

— ISAIAH 7:4

When my heart sinks, it sinks into the quicksand of my own fears and preoccupations, where it can see nothing except itself. When I lift it up to you, it rises into freedom, where it can see your world and your suffering children.

Isaiah 7:1–9
Psalm 48
Matthew 11:20–24

*Jesus said . . . , "I give praise to you, Father, Lord of
heaven and earth, for although you have hidden these
things from the wise and the learned you have revealed them
to the childlike."*

— MATTHEW 11:25

Underneath all the layers of learning and skill
lies a heart that once knew how to marvel at the
simple miracle of life—a heart that once
received life without needing to conquer or
control it, and a heart that can still recapture
that first dawn of wonder.

Isaiah 10:5–7, 13–16
Psalm 94
Matthew 11:25–27

As a woman about to give birth
writhes and cries out in her pains,
so were we in your presence, O LORD.
We conceived and writhed in pain,
giving birth to wind.

— ISAIAH 26:17–18

Once your love has been conceived in our hearts
we have no choice but to bear it into our world.
We consented to the conception, Lord, and we
consent to the pains of labor for the sake of the
coming of your kingdom.

Isaiah 26:7–9, 12, 16–19
Psalm 102
Matthew 11:28–30

Those live whom the LORD protects;
yours . . . the life of my spirit.
You have given me health and life;
thus is my bitterness transformed into peace.

— ISAIAH 38:16–17

More than anything, it was Jim's attentive,
unobtrusive care that kept Mike going through
the long months of depression and despair. Jim
nurtured him as someone would a sickly plant in
need of food and water and light. Once he
recovered, Mike knew that he owed everything
to the friend who had kept his heart alive and
had given him back his spirit.

Isaiah 38:1–8, 21–22
Isaiah 38:10–12, 16
Matthew 12:1–8

Woe to those who plan iniquity,
and work out evil on their couches;
In the morning light they accomplish it.

— MICAH 2:1

When we lie and brood in our own inner
darkness, our worst fears can take over and our
worst intentions can become reality. But when
we surrender ourselves to you in the dark silence
of prayer, your joy can become incarnate and
your dream can be fulfilled.

Micah 2:1–5
Psalm 10
Matthew 12:14–21

The kingdom of heaven is like a mustard seed that a person took and sowed in a field. It is the smallest of all the seeds, yet when full-grown it is the largest of plants. It becomes a large bush, and the "birds of the sky come and dwell in its branches."

— MATTHEW 13:31–32

Our faith springs from the tiniest beginnings. Its growth is your gift to us, given not just for ourselves but so that others might find a home in your love, made visible through ours.

Wisdom 12:13, 16–19
Psalm 86
Romans 8:26–27
Matthew 13:24–43 or 13:24–30

Monday

JULY 22

• SAINT MARY MAGDALENE •

You have been told, O man, what is good,
and what the LORD requires of you:
Only to do the right and to love goodness,
and to walk humbly with your God.

— MICAH 6:8

When we walk humbly with you, we cannot fail
to be touched by your tenderness, and when
your tender love has touched us, truth and
justice are our only options.

Micah 6:1–4, 6–8
Psalm 50
John 20:1–2, 11–18

*But he said in reply . . . "Who is my mother? Who are
my brothers?" And stretching out his hand toward his
disciples, he said, "Here are my mother and my brothers.
For whoever does the will of my heavenly Father is my
brother, and sister, and mother."*

— MATTHEW 12:48 – 50

It is you, Lord, who are refused asylum by a
"friendly" government. It is you who are reduced
to poverty in an affluent society. You, Lord—
our brother and our sister.

Micah 7:14–15, 18–20
Psalm 85
Matthew 12:46–50

Before I formed you in the womb I knew you,
before you were born I dedicated you.

— JEREMIAH 1:5

Bernard grew prize gladiola. Each year he
lovingly planted the bulbs, and for every bulb he
planted he had a vision in his heart of the
perfect flower it would become, nurtured by him
until it revealed the fullness of its still-hidden
mystery.

Jeremiah 1:1, 4–10
Psalm 71
Matthew 13:1–9

Thursday

JULY 25

• SAINT JAMES, APOSTLE •

Then the mother of the sons of Zebedee approached him with
her sons and did him homage, wishing to ask him for
something. He said to her, "What do you wish?" She
answered him, "Command that these two sons of mine sit, one
at your right and the other at your left, in your kingdom."
Jesus said in reply, "You do not know what you are asking.
Can you drink the cup that I am going to drink?"

— MATTHEW 20:20 – 22

Among my friends I often notice that those who
have drunk most deeply of the cup of suffering
are those whose lives seem closest to you.

2 Corinthians 4:7–15
Psalm 126
Matthew 20:20–28

But the seed sown on rich soil is the one who hears the word and understands it, who indeed bears fruit and yields a hundred or sixty or thirtyfold.

— MATTHEW 13:23

The yield of the harvest depends not on the labor of our hands but on the receptiveness of our hearts.

Jeremiah 3:14–17
Jeremiah 31:10–13
Matthew 13:18–23

The kingdom of heaven may be likened to a man who sowed good seed in his field. While everyone was asleep his enemy came and sowed weeds all through the wheat, and then went off. When the crop grew and bore fruit, the weeds appeared as well. The slaves of the householder came to him and said, "Master, did you not sow good seed in your field? Where have the weeds come from?" He answered, "An enemy has done this."

— MATTHEW 13:24 – 28

Like weeds, my persistent fears grow fast and furious, taking over my mind and my heart. Yet it is the sure and steady growth of joy that will have the final word, the good seed of joy that is the original inhabitant and rightful heir of my life's soil and will be its eternal harvest.

Jeremiah 7:1–11
Psalm 84
Matthew 13:24–30

Give your servant, therefore, an understanding heart to judge your people and to distinguish right from wrong.

—1 KINGS 3:9

Decisions may be made in my head, but discernment can happen only in my heart.

1 Kings 3:5, 7–12
Psalm 119
Romans 8:28–30
Matthew 13:44–52

Martha, burdened with much serving, came to him and said, "Lord, do you not care that my sister has left me by myself to do the serving? Tell her to help me." The Lord said to her in reply, "Martha, Martha, you are anxious and worried about many things. There is need of only one thing. Mary has chosen the better part and it will not be taken from her."

— LUKE 10:40 – 42

Sometimes my prayer comes from my Martha: "Lord, I have all these issues in my life, and I don't know how to deal with them." Sometimes my Mary leads me into a different kind of prayer. "Lord, I have all these issues going on, but for just these few moments all I ask is to be quite still with you." It is my Mary prayer that gives me the strength to do the Martha things in my life.

Jeremiah 13:1–11
Deuteronomy 32:18–21
John 11:19–27 or Luke 10:38–42

If I walk out into the field,
look! those slain by the sword;
If I enter the city,
look! those consumed by hunger. . . .
You alone have done all these things.

— JEREMIAH 14:18, 22

Our pangs of hunger make us seek out the food
we need, our pains cause us to look for healing,
our anger makes us work for justice, and our
encounters with evil set us in search of our
redeeming.

Jeremiah 14:17–22
Psalm 79
Matthew 13:36–43

The kingdom of heaven is like a merchant searching for fine pearls. When he finds a pearl of great price, he goes and sells all that he has and buys it.

— MATTHEW 13:45 – 46

The deepest desire of my heart is the one that I will follow, letting go of all the lesser ones. Will it lead me to the fullness of your kingdom or to the bankruptcy of my own?

Jeremiah 15:10, 16–21
Psalm 59
Matthew 13:44–46

I went down to the potter's house and there he was, working at the wheel. Whenever the object of clay which he was making turned out badly in his hand, he tried again, making of the clay another object of whatever sort he pleased. . . . [L]ike clay in the hand of the potter, so are you in my hand.

— JEREMIAH 18:3 – 4, 6

We are held in hands that assure us that every false start is a new beginning and every failure an opportunity for a new creation.

Jeremiah 18:1–6
Psalm 146
Matthew 13:47–53

*Where did this man get such wisdom and mighty deeds? Is
he not the carpenter's son?*

— MATTHEW 13:54 – 55

We strain our eyes to see miracles on our life's
horizon and fail to see them lying on the
doorstep of our own experience.

Jeremiah 26:1–9
Psalm 69
Matthew 13:54–58

For the LORD hears the poor,
does not spurn those in bondage.

— PSALM 69:34

Our circumstances hold us captive, as a fence
surrounds a field. Yet we have a choice: we can
focus on the fence that encloses us or on the
view that our field affords, on the clamor of our
needs or on the Lord who listens.

Jeremiah 26:11–16, 24
Psalm 69
Matthew 14:1–12

All you who are thirsty,
come to the water!
You who have no money,
come, receive grain and eat;
Come, without paying and without cost,
drink wine and milk!

— ISAIAH 55:1

It was quite a culture shock for Jim and Maura, moving from an affluent suburb to a depressed industrial town. In their old home, they had been able to buy everything except companionship. Here in their new home, companionship was what they craved above all else, and they discovered with joy that it was given freely and abundantly by their hard-pressed and often unemployed neighbors.

Isaiah 55:1–3
Psalm 145
Romans 8:35, 37–39
Matthew 14:13–21

• THE DEDICATION OF THE BASILICA OF SAINT MARY IN ROME •

During the fourth watch of the night, he came toward them, walking on the sea. . . . [Jesus] spoke to them, "Take courage, it is I; do not be afraid." . . . Peter got out of the boat and began to walk on the water toward Jesus. But when he saw how [strong] the wind was he became frightened; and, beginning to sink, he cried out, "Lord, save me!" Immediately Jesus stretched out his hand and caught him.

— MATTHEW 14:25, 27, 29 – 31

The long nights often felt like storm-tossed seas to Jean as she lay sleepless, struggling with her anxieties about her failing marriage. It was only when she surrendered herself to prayer that she rose above the waves and found new peace, new courage for tomorrow's choices.

Jeremiah 28:1–17
Psalm 119
Matthew 14:22–36

Tuesday

AUGUST 6

*Then Peter said to Jesus in reply, "Lord, it is good that we
are here. If you wish, I will make three tents here, one for
you, one for Moses, and one for Elijah."*

— MATTHEW 17:4

It was hard to see any connection between the
bird displayed in a cage at the zoo and the
awesome experience of the tropical rain forest
where it had once lived. To contain our visions is
to dilute them and destroy them. To live out their
meanings is to embody them for all creation.

Daniel 7:9–10, 13–14
Psalm 97
2 Peter 1:16–19
Matthew 17:1–9

AUGUST 7

The people that escaped the sword
have found favor in the desert.

— JEREMIAH 31:2

The quarrel with his former friend left Richard
devastated and inwardly bleeding. For months
he existed in an inner desert. Only two things
grew in that desert. One was the choking tangle
of his remorse and his regrets. The other was the
soft, determined flower of your forgiveness and
your peace.

Jeremiah 31:1–7
Jeremiah 31:10–13
Matthew 15:21–28

You are Peter, and upon this rock I will build my church.

— MATTHEW 16:18

The rocks that bruise and batter us are the same rocks on which you are building us up into the people of God.

Jeremiah 31:31–34
Psalm 51
Matthew 16:13–23

What profit would there be for one to gain the whole world and forfeit his life? Or what can one give in exchange for his life?

— MATTHEW 16:26

Let our energies be spent on living and not on building up mere monuments to life.

Nahum 2:1, 3; 3:1–3, 6–7
Deuteronomy 32:35–36, 39, 41
Matthew 16:24–28

*[U]nless a grain of wheat falls to the ground and dies,
it remains just a grain of wheat; but if it dies, it produces
much fruit.*

—JOHN 12:24

When I look back over my soul's journey, I
realize with hindsight that the periods of real
growth and fruitfulness began in the times when
I felt most inwardly alone, chilled and blinded
by the surrounding darkness and stripped of the
outer husks of my former certainties and
securities. A dead seed, ready for new life.

2 Corinthians 9:6–10
Psalm 112
John 12:24–26

After [he dismissed the crowds], he went up on the
mountain by himself to pray. When it was evening he was
there alone. Meanwhile the boat, already a few miles
offshore, was being tossed about by the waves, for the wind
was against it. During the fourth watch of the night, he
came toward them, walking on the sea.

— MATTHEW 14:23–25

I battle against my heavy seas, Lord, and where
are you? You are with the Father, drawing
strength for both of us before coming to me with
your saving grip.

1 Kings 19:9, 11–13
Psalm 85
Romans 9:1–5
Matthew 14:22–33

I saw what looked like fire; he was surrounded with splendor. . . . Such was the vision of the likeness of the glory of the LORD.

— EZEKIEL 1:27–28

If I look back over each day's living, I will find a speck of gold among the grains of sand, a moment in which I have recognized your reality as part of my very identity.

Ezekiel 1:2–5, 24–28
Psalm 148
Matthew 17:22–27

Tuesday

AUGUST 13

• SAINT PONTIAN, POPE AND MARTYR • SAINT HIPPOLYTUS, PRIEST AND
MARTYR •

*He [the Lord] said to me: Son of man, eat what is before
you; eat this scroll, then go, speak to the house of Israel. So
I opened my mouth and he gave me the scroll to eat. Son of
man, he then said to me, feed your belly and fill your
stomach with this scroll I am giving you. I ate it, and it
was as sweet as honey.*

— EZEKIEL 3:1–3

Your word is not for filing in the reference
sections of our head, but for taking into
ourselves and digesting, and for becoming the
truth that feeds us.

Ezekiel 2:8–3:4
Psalm 119
Matthew 18:1–5, 10, 12–14

If he [your brother] refuses to listen even to the church, then
treat him as you would a Gentile or a tax collector.

— MATTHEW 18:17

. . . yet remembering, Lord, that you also treated
the Gentiles and the tax collectors with love.

Ezekiel 9:1–7; 10:18–22
Psalm 113
Matthew 18:15–20

AUGUST 15

• THE ASSUMPTION OF THE BLESSED VIRGIN MARY •

*From now on will all ages call me blessed. The Mighty
One has done great things for me, and holy is his name.
His mercy is from age to age to those who fear him.*

— LUKE 1:48 – 50

When just one of your children acknowledges
your holiness from her heart, it opens up a
spring of blessing that will cascade through the
generations to come.

VIGIL:

1 Chronicles 15:3–4, 15–16; 16:1–2

Psalm 132

1 Corinthians 15:54–57

Luke 11:27–28

DAY:

Revelation 11:19; 12:1–6, 10

Psalm 45

1 Corinthians 15:20–27

Luke 1:39–56

With joy you will draw water
at the fountain of salvation.

— ISAIAH 12:3

The springs of grace that flow in the privacy of
our hearts are deeper than drought and pure
beyond pollution. Private wells, but flowing with
a love that can be shared universally.

Ezekiel 16:1–15, 60, 63 or 16:59–63
Isaiah 12:2–6
Matthew 19:3–12

If a man is virtuous, . . . if he does not defile his neighbor's wife, . . . if he oppresses no one, gives back the pledge received for a debt, commits no robbery; if he gives food to the hungry and clothes the naked; if he does not lend at interest nor exact usury; if he holds off from evildoing, judges fairly between a man and his opponent; if he lives by my statutes and is careful to observe my ordinances . . . he shall surely live, says the Lord GOD.

— EZEKIEL 18:5 – 9

You walked along High Street, looking for an upright man. You stopped at the newsstands and noticed the magazines on the top shelf. You stopped by the homeless man crouched on a doorstep and noticed us hurrying by. You stopped outside the bank and noticed the posters advertising bank loans and credit cards. You stopped outside the police station and noticed the peace demonstrators being herded inside. Then you stopped by the school and watched the crossing guard stop the cars and lead a little child to safety through the hazards of the city traffic, and I knew that you had found what you were looking for.

Ezekiel 18:1–10, 13, 30–32
Psalm 51
Matthew 19:13–15

AUGUST 18

For the gifts and the call of God are irrevocable.

— ROMANS 11:29

It is our own unfaithfulness, Lord, not yours, that
makes us set aside your gifts and falter in
choosing your way.

Isaiah 56:1, 6–7
Psalm 67
Romans 11:13–15, 29–32
Matthew 15:21–28

Son of man, by a sudden blow I am taking away from you
the delight of your eyes, but do not mourn or weep or shed
any tears. Groan in silence, make no lament for the dead.

— EZEKIEL 24:16–17

Let me light a candle in my heart for everything
I have loved and lost. Let the silent tears flow
like softened wax. But let the light of the flame
of hope be the final word and my companion as I
journey forward into life.

Ezekiel 24:15–24
Deuteronomy 32:18–21
Matthew 19:16–22

Then Jesus said to his disciples, "Amen, I say to you, it
will be hard for one who is rich to enter the kingdom of
heaven. Again I say to you, it is easier for a camel to pass
through the eye of a needle than for one who is rich to enter
the kingdom of God."

— MATTHEW 19:23 – 24

The climbers had to leave their rucksacks behind
before setting out for the summit. The most
beautiful and mysterious parts of the mountain
were only accessible through the slimmest of
openings between the rocks, where there was no
room for any baggage.

Ezekiel 28:1–10
Deuteronomy 32:26–28, 30, 35–36
Matthew 19:23–30

You have fed off their milk, worn their wool, and
slaughtered the fatlings, but the sheep you have not
pastured. You did not strengthen the weak nor heal the sick
nor bind up the injured.

— EZEKIEL 34:3 – 4

Forgive us, Lord, for we have shorn you of your
wool and have not even bound the wounds of
that shearing. We have drained you of your milk,
yet we have failed to replenish you. We have
done this to our brothers and sisters, Lord.
We have done this to you.

Ezekiel 34:1–11
Psalm 23
Matthew 20:1–16

⋺ 268 ⋹

I will give you a new heart and place a new spirit within you, taking from your bodies your stony hearts and giving you natural hearts.

— EZEKIEL 36:26

We seek to bypass our hearts using all the defenses and delusions we can muster. Give us the courage to surrender ourselves instead to your transplant operation.

Ezekiel 36:23–28
Psalm 51
Matthew 22:1–14

The hand of the LORD came upon me, and he led me out in the spirit of the LORD and set me in the center of the plain, which was now filled with bones. . . . Then he said to me: "Prophesy over these bones, and say to them: Dry bones, hear the word of the LORD! Thus says the Lord GOD to these bones: See! I will bring spirit into you, that you may come to life. I will put sinews upon you, make flesh grow over you, cover you with skin, and put spirit in you so that you may come to life and know that I am the LORD."

— EZEKIEL 37:1, 4 –7

Hannah was numbed with grief after her life companion died. She sat, day after day, immobilized by sadness and regret, gazing at faded photographs of their childhood and their youth. Until one day the neighbors' little girl knocked on her door with a message from her parents. It was the start of a new friendship. The old lady and the child would sit together and chat, and soon Hannah's faded photographs became a new and living love.

Ezekiel 37:1–14
Psalm 107
Matthew 22:34–40

Philip found Nathanael and told him, "We have found the one about whom Moses wrote in the law, and also the prophets, Jesus, son of Joseph, from Nazareth." But Nathanael said to him, "Can anything good come from Nazareth?"

— JOHN 1:45 – 46

We may block the growth of stranger into friend by refusing to look beneath the surface of his outward appearance or mannerisms.

Revelation 21:9–14
Psalm 145
John 1:45–51

Simon Peter said in reply, "You are the Messiah, the Son of the living God." Jesus said to him in reply, "Blessed are you, Simon son of Jonah. For flesh and blood has not revealed this to you, but my heavenly Father."

— MATTHEW 16:16–17

We spend years of our lives gathering knowledge and understanding from our learning and experience, but the inner certainties of true wisdom come to us unbidden in timeless moments of clarity.

Isaiah 22:19–23
Psalm 138
Romans 11:33–36
Matthew 16:13–20

AUGUST 26

You blind ones, which is greater, the gift, or the altar that makes the gift sacred?

— MATTHEW 23:19

I unwrapped the gift carefully. The beautiful wrapping made it special, but the real specialness was in the love with which you gave it to me.

2 Thessalonians 1:1–5, 11–12
Psalm 96
Matthew 23:13–22

Woe to you, scribes and Pharisees, you hypocrites. You cleanse the outside of cup and dish, but inside they are full of plunder and self-indulgence. Blind Pharisee, cleanse first the inside of the cup, so that the outside also may be clean.

— MATTHEW 23:25 – 26

In your presence, Lord, we are turned inside out. Perhaps that is why we are so hesitant to enter it.

2 Thessalonians 2:1–3, 14–17
Psalm 96
Matthew 23:23–26

This greeting is in my own hand, Paul's. This is the sign in every letter; this is how I write.

— 2 THESSALONIANS 3:17

So you too, Lord, write your name by your own hand in each believer's heart, marking us with the sign of your authenticity and drawing us toward the same genuineness as that which belongs to you, whose name we bear.

2 Thessalonians 3:6–10, 16–18
Psalm 128
Matthew 23:27–32

[Y]ou are not lacking in any spiritual gift as you wait for the revelation of our Lord Jesus Christ.

—1 CORINTHIANS 1:7

All that we need for Christ to be revealed in us is already present in the sometimes unwelcoming soil of our daily circumstances. Everything is a gift with the potential to bring a little of God's love to life in us.

1 Corinthians 1:1–9
Psalm 145
Mark 6:17–29

For Jews demand signs and Greeks look for wisdom, but we proclaim Christ crucified, a stumbling block to Jews and foolishness to Gentiles, but to those who are called, Jews and Greeks alike, Christ the power of God and the wisdom of God.

—1 CORINTHIANS 1:22 – 24

Katy admired David's ability to engage the attention of their friends in what he said and did, and she had great respect for the understanding he revealed in their conversations, but it wasn't until she saw him, weak and broken, in a hospital bed that she knew how much she loved him.

1 Corinthians 1:17–25
Psalm 33
Matthew 25:1–13

*For to everyone who has, more will be given and he will
grow rich; but from the one who has not, even what he has
will be taken away.*

— MATTHEW 25:29

The nudge of inspiration comes quietly, urging
us to exercise a hidden talent and let it bear fruit.
If we respond, it will grow, strengthening our
confidence and ability. If we ignore it, it will fade
and become lost, and we may never know what
gifts we have left buried in the unexplored
depths of our lives.

1 Corinthians 1:26–31
Psalm 33
Matthew 25:14–30

Do not conform yourself to this age but be transformed by the renewal of your mind.

— ROMANS 12:2

Our true shape is not the one imposed on us from the pressures around us but the one that emerges from within us, where you dwell, as a flower emerges from a seed.

Jeremiah 20:7–9
Psalm 63
Romans 12:1–2
Matthew 16:21–27

The Spirit of the Lord is upon me,
because he has anointed me
to bring glad tidings to the poor.
He has sent me to proclaim liberty to captives
and recovery of sight to the blind,
to let the oppressed go free,
and to proclaim a year acceptable to the Lord.

— LUKE 4:18–19

When we offer a word of love to the lonely,
when we take a trembling hand into our own,
when we help a child solve a problem, or when
we intervene to curb a playground fight, we are
sharing your anointing, Lord, and letting your
kingdom show.

1 Corinthians 2:1–5
Psalm 119
Luke 4:16–30

For the Spirit scrutinizes everything, even the depths of God. Among human beings, who knows what pertains to a person except the spirit of the person that is within? Similarly, no one knows what pertains to God except the Spirit of God.

—1 CORINTHIANS 2:10–11

When I seek the depths of my own spirit in prayer, I discover your Spirit waiting to receive me where deep calls to deep.

1 Corinthians 2:10–16
Psalm 145
Luke 4:31–37

I planted, Apollos watered, but God caused the growth.
Therefore, neither the one who plants nor the one who
waters is anything, but only God, who causes the growth.

—1 CORINTHIANS 3:6–7

Without your seed, all our planting would be
futile. Without your power of growth, all our
cultivation would be in vain. Let our work serve
your life, and may our lives be lived in the
presence of the One who makes us grow.

1 Corinthians 3:1–9
Psalm 33
Luke 4:38–44

*Paul or Apollos or Kephas, or the world or life or death, or
the present or the future: all belong to you, and you to
Christ, and Christ to God.*

—1 CORINTHIANS 3:22 – 23

Time, and all that it brings to us and takes away
again, is just a stream in which we flow home to
fullness.

1 Corinthians 3:18–23
Psalm 24
Luke 5:1–11

*He [the Lord] will bring to light what is hidden in darkness
and will manifest the motives of our hearts.*

—1 CORINTHIANS 4:5

If we could see each others' hearts as God sees
us, we might be surprised to see the selfish
motives that sometimes prompt our generosity
and the love that is often buried beneath our
worst mistakes.

1 Corinthians 4:1–5
Psalm 37
Luke 5:33–39

While he was going through a field of grain on a sabbath,
his disciples were picking the heads of grain, rubbing them
in their hands, and eating them. Some Pharisees said,
"Why are you doing what is unlawful on the sabbath?"
Jesus said to them in reply, . . . "The Son of Man is lord
of the sabbath."

— LUKE 6:1–2, 5

Forgive us, Lord, when the complications we
impose on ourselves and on each other prevent
us from simply living.

1 Corinthians 4:6–15
Psalm 145
Luke 6:1–5

*For where two or three are gathered together in my name,
there am I in the midst of them.*

— MATTHEW 18:20

When your love flows through our human circles,
the circles become mirrors of your trinity—each
is bound to all and all to each, and every circle is
centered on you.

Ezekiel 33:7–9
Psalm 95
Romans 13:8–10
Matthew 18:15–20

*On another sabbath he went into the synagogue and
taught, and there was a man there whose right hand was
withered. . . . [Jesus] then said to him, "Stretch out your
hand." He did so and his hand was restored.*

— LUKE 6:6, 10

The broken one who reaches out to you for
healing is already halfway to wholeness.

1 Corinthians 5:1–8
Psalm 5
Luke 6:6–11

⇒ 288 ⇐

SEPTEMBER 10

*In those days he departed to the mountain to pray, and he
spent the night in prayer to God. When day came, he
called his disciples to himself, and from them he chose
Twelve, whom he also named apostles.*

— LUKE 6:12–13

If every decision we made were preceded by a
night of prayer—if every daylight choice were
shaped by your presence in our darkness—how
different our lives might be.

1 Corinthians 6:1–11
Psalm 149
Luke 6:12–19

Blessed are you who are now hungry,
for you will be satisfied.

— LUKE 6:21

Jack had never known hunger. Long years of
business lunches had dulled his appetite and had
taken a terrible toll on his heart. Now, just out of
intensive care, he took the glass of water from
the nurse's hand, and nothing in the world had
ever tasted so good.

1 Corinthians 7:25–31
Psalm 45
Luke 6:20–26

SEPTEMBER 12

Be merciful, just as [also] your Father is merciful. Stop judging and you will not be judged. Stop condemning and you will not be condemned. Forgive and you will be forgiven.

— LUKE 6:36 – 37

Marion used to criticize every other driver on the road, until one day her small son said, "But you do that too, Mom." It was a moment of truth, and the remarkable thing was that when she stopped criticizing others, she had more energy to concentrate on being a better driver herself.

1 Corinthians 8:1–7, 11–13
Psalm 139
Luke 6:27–38

Can a blind person guide a blind person? Will not both fall into a pit?

— LUKE 6:39

The pits open up in front of us when we try to lead each other. The way is much safer if we remain humbly alongside each other, equally in need of and dependent on you.

1 Corinthians 9:16–19, 22–27
Psalm 84
Luke 6:39–42

For God did not send his Son into the world to condemn the world, but that the world might be saved through him.

— JOHN 3:17

Each thought or word of judgment undermines your kingdom, Lord. Every gesture of affirmation and encouragement builds it up.

Numbers 21:4–9
Psalm 78
Philippians 2:6–11
John 3:13–17

⋺ 293 ⋲

Then Peter approaching asked him, "Lord, if my brother sins against me, how often must I forgive him? As many as seven times?" Jesus answered, "I say to you, not seven times but seventy-seven times."

— MATTHEW 18:21–22

Just when I thought I had finally forgiven him, a chance remark awakened all my old resentments. How deep must my forgiveness go, Lord? From the quiver on my lips through the tears in my eyes and right down to the gash in my heart!

Sirach 27:30–28:9
Psalm 103
Romans 14:7–9
Matthew 18:21–35

• SAINT CORNELIUS, POPE AND MARTYR • SAINT CYPRIAN OF CARTHAGE,
BISHOP AND MARTYR •

Sacrifice and offering you do not want;
but ears open to obedience you gave me.
Holocausts and sin-offerings you do not require;
so I said, "Here I am."

— PSALM 40:7– 8

As long as I bring you my own sacrifices, my
own offerings, I keep my relationship with you
under my control. When I bring you my self and
my unconditional attentiveness, I hand over that
control to you.

1 Corinthians 11:17–26, 33
Psalm 40
Luke 7:1–10

He stepped forward and touched the coffin; at this the
bearers halted, and he said, "Young man, I tell you, arise!"
The dead man sat up and began to speak, and Jesus gave
him to his mother.

— LUKE 7:14 –15

When you touch our frozen hearts and draw us
back into the fullness of life in you, you do it not
just for our own sake but in order to give us back
to the world, charged with your living Spirit.

1 Corinthians 12:12–14, 27–31
Psalm 100
Luke 7:11–17

⊰ 296 ⊱

At present we see indistinctly, as in a mirror, but then face to face. At present I know partially; then I shall know fully, as I am fully known.

—1 CORINTHIANS 13:12

When I stop looking at my own mirror image and turn instead to look into your face, then, at last, in your clear, love-filled gaze, I will see your promise of who I really am.

1 Corinthians 12:31–13:13
Psalm 33
Luke 7:31–35

*Then [Jesus] . . . said to Simon, "Do you see this woman?
. . . I tell you, her many sins have been forgiven; hence, she
has shown great love. But the one to whom little is forgiven,
loves little."*

— LUKE 7:44, 47

If we are tempted to feel that we love you more
than others do, help us to remember, Lord, that
the measure of our love for you is the measure of
the forgiveness you have poured out upon us,
and the measure of that forgiveness is the
measure of our need of it.

1 Corinthians 15:1–11
Psalm 118
Luke 7:36–50

• SAINTS ANDREW KIM TAEGON, PRIEST AND MARTYR, AND PAUL CHONG
HASANG, MARTYR, AND THEIR COMPANIONS, MARTYRS •

Hide me in the shadow of your wings.

— PSALM 17:8

When I feel weak, I run to you for shelter, as a
chick runs to the mother hen. When I feel
strong, let me not forget that it is your eagle's
wings that are carrying me above the storm.

1 Corinthians 15:12–20
Psalm 17
Luke 8:1–3

The Pharisees saw this and said to his disciples, "Why does your teacher eat with tax collectors and sinners?" He heard this and said, "Those who are well do not need a physician, but the sick do."

— MATTHEW 9:11–12

The doctor we need is the one who comes to us where we are and then sends us to be with others where they are.

Ephesians 4:1–7, 11–13
Psalm 19
Matthew 9:9–13

SEPTEMBER 22

For my thoughts are not your thoughts,
nor are your ways my ways, says the LORD.
As high as the heavens are above the earth,
so high are my ways above your ways
and my thoughts above your thoughts.

— ISAIAH 55 : 8 – 9

My image of you is as far removed from your
reality as a pinpoint of starlight in the night sky
is removed from the fiery sun that is its source—
yet both my image and your reality shine with
the same light, and it is only my distance from
you that makes the difference.

Isaiah 55:6–9
Psalm 145
Philippians 1:20–24, 27
Matthew 20:1–16

Say not to your neighbor, "Go, and come again,
tomorrow I will give," when you can give at once.
— PROVERBS 3:28

Mary had to pass old Hannah's door every day
when she came home from work. During the
cold snap she wondered whether Hannah was
keeping warm enough and if perhaps she should
go over and check on her. Then one evening
Mary saw a police car and an ambulance parked
outside. The finality of death had frozen her
good intentions into inescapable regret.

Proverbs 3:27–34
Psalm 15
Luke 8:16–18

SEPTEMBER 24

All the ways of a man may be right in his own eyes,
but it is the LORD who proves hearts.

— PROVERBS 21:2

The leadenness of sorrow and pain can add
weight and substance to our hearts that the
feathers of mere pleasure can never bring.

Proverbs 21:1–6, 10–13
Psalm 119
Luke 8:19–21

*And as for those who do not welcome you, when you leave
that town, shake the dust from your feet in testimony
against them.*

— LUKE 9:5

The dust of old hurts and resentments
accumulates and clings to my feet like a solid
layer of mud, until it finally prevents me from
moving on at all. To shake it off is to set myself,
and those who caused the hurting, free.

Proverbs 30:5–9
Psalm 119
Luke 9:1–6

Humans disappear like sleep at dawn;
they are like grass that dies.
In sprouts green in the morning;
by evening it is dry and withered.

— PSALM 90:5 – 6

When we acknowledge the transience of life and
are content to let ourselves become a space
through which life flows, we begin to grasp the
meaning of eternity.

Ecclesiastes 1:2–11
Psalm 90:3–6, 12–14, 17
Luke 9:7–9

⋙ 305 ⋘

There is an appointed time for everything,
and a time for every affair under the heavens.
A time to be born, and a time to die;
a time to plant, and a time to uproot the plant. . . .
A time to scatter stones, and a time to gather them. . . .
A time to seek, and a time to lose;
a time to keep, and a time to cast away.

— ECCLESIASTES 3:1–2, 5

Bill and Emma had grown old together—he the dominant decision maker, she the meek peacemaker. Now he was helpless and dependent in his infirmity, and she marveled at his newfound calmness while she discovered in herself a new strength of leadership in the life of the community. There are times and seasons for growth and change and for discovering new and surprising depths and breadths of personality.

Ecclesiastes 3:1–11
Psalm 144
Luke 9:18–22

When the almond tree blooms,
and the locust grows sluggish
and the caper berry is without effect,
Because man goes to his lasting home.

— ECCLESIASTES 12:5

The village cemetery was alive with cherry
blossoms and daffodils. Burgeoning life in the
midst of the monuments of death. In this place it
was impossible to believe that death could have
the final word.

Ecclesiastes 11:9–12:8
Psalm 90
Luke 9:43–45

A man had two sons. He came to the first and said, "Son, go out and work in the vineyard today." He said in reply, "I will not," but afterwards he changed his mind and went. The man came to the other son and gave the same order. He said in reply, "Yes, sir," but did not go. Which of the two did his father's will?

— MATTHEW 21:28 – 31

Janet worried about her rebellious daughter, who adamantly refused to go to church with the rest of the family. Years later, when Janet's obedient children had long since strayed from their faith, she recognized her daughter's deep, abiding love of God and her commitment to those in need around her.

Ezekiel 18:25–28
Psalm 25
Philippians 2:1–11 or 2:1–5
Matthew 21:28–32

Naked I came forth from my mother's womb,
and naked shall I go back again.
The LORD gave and the LORD has taken away;
blessed be the name of the LORD!

— JOB 1:21

When gain and loss become as commonplace as
breathing in and breathing out, we will begin to
see how close you were to us when we thought
we were most grievously alone.

Job 1:6–22
Psalm 17
Luke 9:46–50

OCTOBER 1

• SAINT THÉRÈSE OF THE CHILD JESUS, VIRGIN AND DOCTOR OF THE CHURCH •

LORD, my God, I call out by day;
at night I cry aloud in your presence.
Let my prayer come before you;
incline your ear to my cry.

— PSALM 88:2 – 3

I beg you to receive my prayer into your
presence, and you respond by opening my heart
to your presence in my prayer.

Job 3:1–3, 11–17, 20–23
Psalm 88
Luke 9:51–56

See that you do not despise one of these little ones, for I say to you that their angels in heaven always look upon the face of my heavenly Father.

— MATTHEW 18:10

Truth shines out of every little child until the solid outer shells of defensiveness and selfishness begin to thicken and obscure the light. We must cherish our little ones, light carriers, truth tellers, for their wisdom may outweigh all our knowledge.

Job 9:1–12, 14–16
Psalm 88
Matthew 18:1–5, 10

Thursday

OCTOBER 3

The harvest is abundant but the laborers are few; so ask the
master of the harvest to send out laborers for his harvest.

— LUKE 10:2

When we pray to you to call more people to
your service, give us the grace to hear the ways
in which you are calling us.

Job 19:21–27
Psalm 27
Luke 10:1–12

LORD, you have probed me, you know me:
you know when I sit and stand;
you understand my thoughts from afar.
My travels and my rest you mark;
with all my ways you are familiar.

— PSALM 139:1– 3

I was once filled with apprehension, knowing that nothing I could do or say or think could be concealed from you. Now I am filled with hope and trust, knowing that whatever path I take, it has the potential to lead me to you.

Job 38:1, 12–21; 40:3–5
Psalm 139
Luke 10:13–16

Then Job died, old and full of years.

— JOB 42:17

To die an old man is one thing, but to have lived a life in which every day was really lived, that is quite another.

Job 42:1–3, 5–6, 12–17
Psalm 119
Luke 10:17–24

---

*Have no anxiety at all, but in everything, by prayer and
petition, with thanksgiving, make your requests known to
God. Then the peace of God that surpasses all understanding
will guard your hearts and minds in Christ Jesus.*

— PHILIPPIANS 4:6–7

We cling to our ways of peace by staying on the
outer edges of life's confrontations, but your
peace is right at their center. It is the axis around
which our whole being, with all its needs and
sorrows, spins.

Isaiah 5:1–7
Psalm 80
Philippians 4:6–9
Matthew 21:33–43

But a Samaritan traveler who came upon him was moved
with compassion at the sight. He approached the victim,
poured oil and wine over his wounds and bandaged them.
Then he lifted him up on his own animal, took him to an
inn and cared for him.

— LUKE 10:33 – 34

A crowd of bystanders gathered around the scene of the accident. They watched the paramedics carrying the old woman to the ambulance, and they were relieved that none of their own family had been involved. In the emergency ward the nurses did all they could to ease her pain and bind her wounds, but they ran out of the time and money they needed to care for her properly. When she was sent home, the immigrant family from next door came over. They turned their compassion into daily unobtrusive care of their wounded neighbor.

Galatians 1:6–12
Psalm 111
Luke 10:25–37

The Lord said to her in reply, "Martha, Martha, you are anxious and worried about many things. There is need of only one thing."

— LUKE 10:41–42

We are anxious for so much that is out of reach, when all we really need is waiting to be claimed by us in the treasure of the present moment.

Galatians 1:13–24
Psalm 139
Luke 10:38–42

• SAINT DENIS, BISHOP AND MARTYR, AND HIS COMPANIONS, MARTYRS •
SAINT JOHN LEONARDI, PRIEST •

Lord, teach us to pray.

— LUKE 11:1

When we teach our children about our world,
we give them something of our knowledge.
When you teach us how to pray, you give us
something of yourself.

Galatians 2:1–2, 7–14
Psalm 117
Luke 11:1–4

And I tell you, ask and you will receive; seek and you will find; knock and the door will be opened to you.

— LUKE 11:9

Lord, give us the courage to ask you for what we most desire so that we may hear ourselves acknowledge our deepest needs and most fervent hopes in your presence. And, in acknowledging them, may we open ourselves up to your fulfilling of them.

Galatians 3:1–5
Luke 1:69–75
Luke 11:5–13

I will praise the LORD with all my heart
in the assembled congregation of the upright.
Great are the works of the LORD,
to be treasured for all their delights.

— PSALM 111:1–2

To hear the parish gossips talking, you might think that everything was wrong with the church. Their criticism ranged from that of the vicar to the altar flowers, from the liturgy to the summer festival. Maeve stayed behind to be alone in prayer. She was confused by their criticisms of the church, yet surely it was in this place, among these people, that she had found her way home to God! As she prayed, her perspective on the parish critics became clear, and her heart expanded with the love that bound them to each other, in spite of themselves.

Galatians 3:7–14
Psalm 111
Luke 11:15–26

Saturday

OCTOBER 12

*For through faith you are all children of God in Christ
Jesus. For all of you who were baptized into Christ have
clothed yourselves with Christ.*

— GALATIANS 3:26 – 27

When I am dressed for a ball, I don't go wading
through the mud. Lord, may the ways of my
heart and the pattern of my living become
consistent with the words in which I clothe my
faith.

Galatians 3:22–29
Psalm 105
Luke 11:27–28

Then he [the king] said to his servants, "The feast is ready, but those who were invited were not worthy to come. Go out, therefore, into the main roads and invite to the feast whomever you find." The servants went out into the streets and gathered all they found, bad and good alike, and the hall was filled with guests.

— MATTHEW 22:8–10

We may be very surprised by some of the unlikely people you have invited to your feast—but they may be even more surprised to find us there!

Isaiah 25:6–10
Psalm 23
Philippians 4:12–14, 19–20
Matthew 22:1–14 or 22:1–10

Monday

OCTOBER 14

• COLUMBUS DAY • SAINT CALLISTUS I, POPE AND MARTYR •

*For freedom Christ set us free; so stand firm and do not
submit again to the yoke of slavery.*

— GALATIANS 5:1

Barbara caught the cat and gently took the
terrified little bird from the cat's jaws. As she
carried the bird to a safe place and let it fly free,
she realized that it would need strength,
courage, and constant vigilance to stay free and
to live.

Galatians 4:22–24, 26–27, 31–5:1
Psalm 113
Luke 11:29–32

You are separated from Christ, you who are trying to be justified by law; you have fallen from grace. . . . For in Christ Jesus . . . only faith working through love [counts for anything].

— GALATIANS 5:4, 6

Every time I think I have managed, by my own efforts, to act in accordance with your will, I move a little bit farther away from that helpless acknowledgement of my utter need of you, which alone can break me open to your love.

Galatians 5:1–6
Psalm 119
Luke 11:37–41

In contrast, the fruit of the Spirit is love, joy, peace, patience,
kindness, generosity, faithfulness, gentleness, self-control.

— GALATIANS 5:22 – 23

Paul and Monica registered for their wedding
early, and the appliances, towels, and linens duly
arrived from friends and relatives. But the gifts
that came silently and unseen, through the
sacrament of their vows, were altogether
different and much more necessary.

Galatians 5:18–25
Psalm 1
Luke 11:42–46

Thursday

OCTOBER 17

• SAINT IGNATIUS OF ANTIOCH, BISHOP AND MARTYR •

*Woe to you! You build the memorials of the prophets whom
your ancestors killed. Consequently, you bear witness and
give consent to the deeds of your ancestors, for they killed
them and you do the building.*

— LUKE 11:47–48

Reg never talked about the war. He even tried to
avoid thinking about it. But sometimes his walks
would bring him face to face with the war
memorial, the fine marble structure that listed
the names of his friends who had been pitched
along with him into wholesale slaughter. When
this happened, he would flinch inwardly,
swallow his anger and his grief, and walk
resolutely in the opposite direction.

Ephesians 1:1–10
Psalm 98
Luke 11:47–54

---

*I am sending you like lambs among wolves. Carry no
money bag, no sack, no sandals.*

— LUKE 10:3 – 4

When I carry nothing, I am freed of the fear of
loss, and there is space in my heart and in my
life through which your love can flow.

2 Timothy 4:10–17
Psalm 145
Luke 10:1–9

OCTOBER 19

*May the eyes of [your] hearts be enlightened, that you
may know what is the hope that belongs to his call.*

— EPHESIANS 1:18

The light of your hope, like the light of the
stars, shines most brightly through our deepest
darkness. It may seem so distant, yet it is the truest
beacon through and companion of our night.

Ephesians 1:15–23
Psalm 8
Luke 12:8–12

For our gospel did not come to you in word alone, but also in power and in the holy Spirit and [with] much conviction.

—1 THESSALONIANS 1:5

Janice rarely speaks directly of her faith. But in the quiet authority of the life she lives in you, those who know her know that they are touching one who is in touch with you, one through whom the currents of your love are flowing.

Isaiah 45:1, 4–6
Psalm 96
1 Thessalonians 1:1–5
Matthew 22:15–21

For we are his handiwork, created in Christ Jesus for the good works that God has prepared in advance, that we should live in them.

— EPHESIANS 2:10

The old painting had been buried in the vaults for long-forgotten years, yet in the hands of the restorers it was cleaned and touched up until the full glory of the artist's first intention shone from the canvas. It was a unique expression of his mind and heart, and the world had been incomplete without it.

Ephesians 2:1–10
Psalm 100
Luke 12:13–21

*For he is our peace, he who made both one and broke down
the dividing wall of enmity, through his flesh.*

— EPHESIANS 2:14

May we kill nothing but that which kills the
wholeness of another. May we destroy nothing
but the barriers that divide us.

Ephesians 2:12–22
Psalm 85
Luke 12:35–38

⇒ 334 ⇐

OCTOBER 23

Much will be required of the person entrusted with much, and still more will be demanded of the person entrusted with more.

— LUKE 12:48

Diane knew that the brightest and most gifted children in her class of eight-year-olds could be prone to boredom, so she sometimes asked them to help the slower children with their reading and writing. They passed their own skills on to their classmates, and in return they learned patience and responsibility. It was a sharing of gifts that helped to transform the class into a real community.

Ephesians 3:2–12
Isaiah 12:2–6
Luke 12:39–48

*For this reason I kneel before the Father . . . that he may
grant you in accord with the riches of his glory to be
strengthened with power through his Spirit in the inner self,
and that Christ may dwell in your hearts through faith;
that you, rooted and grounded in love, may have strength
to comprehend with all the holy ones what is the breadth
and length and height and depth.*

— EPHESIANS 3:14, 16 –18

The soil of our circumstances, which sometimes
seems so hostile to our growth, is the very place—
and the only place—where our hidden roots
find the nutrients that keep them in being and
lead in time to the realization of the full height
and breadth of our life's flowering and fruiting.

Ephesians 3:14–21
Psalm 33
Luke 12:49–53

---

*You know how to interpret the appearance of the earth and the
sky; why do you not know how to interpret the present time?*

— LUKE 12:56

We are so immersed in the laboratory of human
knowledge that we sometimes forget to look out
the window and see what is actually happening
to us. Lord, take our knowledge and transform it
into wisdom.

Ephesians 4:1–6
Psalm 24
Luke 12:54–59

Living the truth in love, we should grow in every way into him who is the head.

— EPHESIANS 4:15

When we live out the dream you have planted in our hearts, discerning it gradually in the light of your truth and your love, we will become who you are calling us to become as surely as the acorn becomes an oak.

Ephesians 4:7–16
Psalm 122
Luke 13:1–9

You shall love the Lord, your God, with all your heart, with all your soul, and with all your mind. This is the greatest and the first commandment. The second is like it: You shall love your neighbor as yourself. The whole law and the prophets depend on these two commandments.

— MATTHEW 22:37–40

Love is not an optional extra, something that warms and softens our ways of living and relating; rather, our ways of living and relating are the ways in which the Love that holds us in being is given its incarnate expression.

Exodus 22:20–26
Psalm 18
1 Thessalonians 1:5–10
Matthew 22:34–40

⇒ 339 ⇐

*So then you are no longer strangers and sojourners, but
you are fellow citizens with the holy ones and members of
the household of God, built upon the foundation of the
apostles and prophets, with Jesus Christ himself as the
capstone. . . . [I]n him you also are being built together
into a dwelling place of God in the Spirit.*

— EPHESIANS 2:19 – 20, 22

No living creature can be excluded from a house
where God lives. There is room for everything
in a house of wholeness.

Ephesians 2:19–22
Psalm 19
Luke 6:12–16

OCTOBER 29

For no one hates his own flesh but rather nourishes and cherishes it, even as Christ does the church, because we are members of his body.

— EPHESIANS 5:29 – 30

With gentle, careful hands, I dressed the wound on my foot. Why am I, a living cell of your body, not just as gentle and careful when attending to the needs and wounds of your other living cells?

Ephesians 5:21–33 or 5:25–33
Psalm 128
Luke 13:18–21

OCTOBER 30

[B]e obedient to your human masters with fear and trembling . . . willingly serving the Lord and not human beings.

— EPHESIANS 6:5, 7

Little Tricia dragged her feet and dawdled and pulled with all her weight against her mother's urging. She had no desire to go shopping. In the afternoon, she skipped lightly and buoyantly all the way to the park. It was the difference between duty and delight.

Ephesians 6:1–9
Psalm 145
Luke 13:22–30

*Jerusalem, Jerusalem . . . how many times I yearned to
gather your children together as a hen gathers her brood
under her wings, but you were unwilling!*

— LUKE 13:34

The mother mallard quickly tried to gather her
six ducklings together in safety when she sensed
the vibrations of the approaching motorboat.
One of them refused. And then there were five.

Ephesians 6:10–20
Psalm 144
Luke 13:31–35

These are the ones who have survived the time of great distress; they have washed their robes and made them white in the blood of the Lamb.

— REVELATION 7:14

Your saints, Lord, are not those who have never failed and fallen, but those who have had the honesty and courage to face their fallenness, admit their need of you, and let your love cleanse them.

Revelation 7:2–4, 9–14
Psalm 24
1 John 3:1–3
Matthew 5:1–12

If, then, we have died with Christ, we believe that we shall also live with him.

— ROMANS 6:8

What a rich comfort it is to know that we dwell not only with Christ but also with all those brothers and sisters who have preceded us in both life and death.

Daniel 12:1–3
Psalm 27
Romans 6:3–9 or 6:3–4, 8–9
John 6:37–40 or any readings taken from Masses for the Dead, nos. 1011–1016

I have stilled my soul,
hushed it like a weaned child.
Like a weaned child on its mother's lap,
so is my soul within me.

— PSALM 131:2

She was only three months old; she was
incontinent and inarticulate and utterly dependent
on me. Yet, as I held her in my arms, she taught
me more about trust and faith than I could ever
begin to understand, let alone teach her.

Malachi 1:14–2:2, 8–10
Psalm 131
1 Thessalonians 2:7–9, 13
Matthew 23:1–12

*Complete my joy by being of the same mind, with the same
love, united in heart, thinking one thing.*

— PHILIPPIANS 2:2

Your love is the apex of our lives and our
desiring. It brings us all together, however far
apart our starting points may be.

Philippians 2:1–4
Psalm 131
Luke 14:12–14

Tuesday

NOVEMBER 5

• ELECTION DAY •

*When the time for the dinner came, he dispatched his servant
to say to those invited, "Come, everything is now ready."
But one by one, they all began to excuse themselves.*

— LUKE 14:17–18

The ingenuity with which I try to avoid what
will make me whole and the tenacity with which
I resist my own redemption always amazes me.

Philippians 2:5–11
Psalm 22
Luke 14:15–24

⋛ 348 ⋚

NOVEMBER 6

You shine like lights in the world, as you hold on to the word of life.

— PHILIPPIANS 2:15 –16

When we offer our friends occasional favors, we may win brief popularity, but when we share with them our friendship with you, your love will flood their lives with light.

Philippians 2:12–18
Psalm 27
Luke 14:25–33

⇒ 349 ⇐

I tell you . . . there will be more joy in heaven over one sinner who repents than over ninety-nine righteous people who have no need of repentance.

— LUKE 15:7

Jim's eyes filled with tears as he embraced his brother at the airport. Twenty-five years of sulky resentment melted away. It was as if their quarrel had never happened. The joy of this homecoming outshone the steady glow of more trouble-free relationships, yet even as it outshone them, it completed and fulfilled them.

Philippians 3:3–8
Psalm 105
Luke 15:1–10

I rejoiced when they said to me,
"Let us go to the house of the LORD."
And now our feet are standing
within your gates, Jerusalem.

— PSALM 122:1–2

Prayer begins with the first quiver of desire to
spend time in your presence, and before we
know what has happened, we are guests in your
heart and pilgrims in your kingdom.

Philippians 3:17–4:1
Psalm 122
Luke 16:1–8

He made a whip out of cords and drove them all out of the temple area, with the sheep and oxen, and spilled the coins of the money-changers and overturned their tables, and to those who sold doves he said, "Take these out of here, and stop making my Father's house a marketplace."

— JOHN 2:15 –16

In the marketplace of life one commodity stands apart from all the rest—your love has no price tag. And at the end of the day, when the market stalls have been dismantled, that one commodity will still be there, because however many people have drawn on it, there is always more.

Ezekiel 47:1–2, 8–9, 12
Psalm 84
1 Corinthians 3:9–11, 16–17
John 2:13–22 or any readings taken from the
Common of the Dedication of a Church, nos. 701–706

Since the bridegroom was long delayed, [the virgins] all became drowsy and fell asleep. At midnight, there was a cry, "Behold, the bridegroom! Come out to meet him!"

— MATTHEW 25:5 – 6

In all our doing and arranging, let us not forget your deeper call to us to live in grace-filled waiting.

Wisdom 6:12–16
Psalm 63
1 Thessalonians 4:13–18 or 4:13–14
Matthew 25:1–13

And the apostles said to the Lord, "Increase our faith." The Lord replied, "If you have faith the size of a mustard seed, you would say to [this] mulberry tree, 'Be uprooted and planted in the sea,' and it would obey you."

— LUKE 17:5 – 6

The faith that we hold as our own is the seed you have sown in our hearts. You are its source of life and growth. We can only watch in wonder as its fullness unfolds.

Titus 1:1–9
Psalm 24
Luke 17:1–6

⋛ 354 ⋛

NOVEMBER 12

• SAINT JOSAPHAT, BISHOP AND MARTYR •

For the grace of God has appeared, saving all and training us to reject godless ways and worldly desires and to live temperately, justly, and devoutly in this age.

— TITUS 2:11–12

When our desire for you is so strong that we can allow nothing to distract us from you, we will again find that all we thought we had lost and surrendered has been made perfect in your love.

Titus 2:1–8, 11–14
Psalm 37
Luke 17:7–10

As he was entering a village, ten lepers met [him]. They stood at a distance from him and raised their voice, saying, "Jesus, Master! Have pity on us!" And when he saw them, he said, "Go show yourselves to the priests." As they were going they were cleansed.

— LUKE 17:12 –14

We call to you for help from afar, hardly daring to approach you. Our healing begins when we hear your response, do as you bid us to do, and then walk on into the future with the courage that comes from trusting that our prayer has been answered.

Titus 3:1–7
Psalm 23
Luke 17:11–19

⇒ 356 ⇐

For just as lightning flashes and lights up the sky from one side to the other, so will the Son of Man be [in his day].

— LUKE 17:24

It was impossible to pinpoint the source of the flash at the center of the storm, but its invisible power caused it to light up the fields and the forests all around us and reveal their every detail. In the same way, the unseen flash point of your love lights up our darkest corners and kindles a fire in our hearts that then glows and flares far beyond the limits of our own lives and our imagination.

Philemon 7–20
Psalm 146
Luke 17:20–25

Whoever seeks to preserve his life will lose it, but whoever loses it will save it.

— LUKE 17:33

Lydia refused to get into the lifeboat without her bag of valuables. Her fellow passengers, shivering and bereft of their possessions, were rowed to safety. Lydia still lies, with her treasure, in the wreckage on the ocean bed.

2 John 4–9
Psalm 119
Luke 17:26–37

Happy are those who fear the LORD. . . .
They shine through the darkness, a light for the upright.

— PSALM 112:1, 4

The first flickering light of our faith seems to
reveal the intensity of the darkness all the more
starkly. Remind us then, Lord, that as soon as
even the most fragile of fires is kindled, the grip
of the darkness has already been broken.

3 John 5–8
Psalm 112
Luke 18:1–8

*Since you were faithful in small matters, I will give you
great responsibilities. Come, share your master's joy.*

— MATTHEW 25:21

Ruth's feelings had been hurt one day in the
office many years ago by an unjust reprimand,
and Elaine had helped ease her hurt by resting
her hand on her colleague's arm in a gesture of
understanding. Today, as Ruth reeled from the
shock of the diagnosis of her terminal illness, she
remembered that gesture of love, and suddenly
she knew who to turn to in her need and in her
loneliness.

Proverbs 31:10–13, 19–20, 30–31
Psalm 128
1 Thessalonians 5:1–6
Matthew 25:14–30 or 25:14–15, 19–21

• DEDICATION OF THE BASILICAS OF THE APOSTLES PETER AND PAUL IN
ROME • SAINT ROSE PHILIPPINE DUCHESNE, VIRGIN •

*I know your works, your labor, and your endurance, and
that you cannot tolerate the wicked. . . . Yet I hold this
against you: you have lost the love you had at first.
Realize how far you have fallen. Repent, and do the works
you did at first.*

— REVELATION 2:2, 4 – 5

The home they had built as a love nest had
become a chore, and the garden had become a
backache. The children had become a worry,
and God himself had become a Sunday
observance. So much work, so much to put up
with—yet underneath it all, everything was
waiting to be rediscovered.

Revelation 1:1–4; 2:1–5
Psalm 1
Luke 18:35–43 or (for the memorial of the dedication) Acts 28:11–16, 30–31
Matthew 14:22–33

*Behold, I stand at the door and knock. If anyone hears my
voice and opens the door, [then] I will enter his house and
dine with him, and he with me.*

— REVELATION 3:20

Only a door divides us, Lord. Only a door stands
between my loneliness and your love. Only a
door . . . and the handle is on my side.

Revelation 3:1–6, 14–22
Psalm 15
Luke 19:1–10

Let everything that has breath
give praise to the LORD!
Hallelujah!

— PSALM 150:6

Remind us, Lord, that when we walk through
our gardens and along our streets, we are moving
through a hallowed cathedral where a service is
always in progress.

Revelation 4:1–11
Psalm 150
Luke 19:11–28

As he drew near [Jerusalem], he saw the city and wept over it, saying, "If this day you only knew what makes for peace—but now it is hidden from your eyes. For the days are coming upon you when your enemies will raise a palisade against you; they will encircle you and hem you in on all sides. They will smash you to the ground and your children within you, and they will not leave one stone upon another within you because you did not recognize the time of your visitation."

— LUKE 19:41–44

The uneasy cease-fire seemed to have ended, and the people of the war-torn city lived in fear again. At a crucial moment in the peace talks, the demons of revenge had broken loose and the opportunity for peace had been lost, perhaps forever. And your tears flow, mingling with ours.

Revelation 5:1–10
Psalm 149
Luke 19:41–44

The chief priests, the scribes, and the leaders of the people, meanwhile, were seeking to put him to death, but they could find no way to accomplish their purpose because all the people were hanging on his words.

— LUKE 19:47–48

We are your people, Lord, and while we hold on to your word, implanted in our hearts, no power on earth can do away with your truth, incarnate in our lives.

Revelation 10:8–11
Psalm 119
Luke 19:45–48

NOVEMBER 23

• SAINT CLEMENT I, POPE AND MARTYR • SAINT COLUMBANUS, ABBOT •
• BLESSED MIGUEL AGUSTÍN PRO, PRIEST AND MARTYR •

He is not God of the dead, but of the living, for to him all are alive.

— LUKE 20:38

The sun and the rain alike nourish the garden in every season as if they know, with a wisdom more profound than ours, that the apparent death of winter is just the cradle of spring.

Revelation 11:4–12
Psalm 144
Luke 20:27–40

*For thus says the Lord GOD: I myself will look after and
tend my sheep. . . . I will rescue them from every place
where they were scattered when it was cloudy and dark.*

— EZEKIEL 34:11–12

When you seem far away and high above us,
Shepherd-Friend, remind us that it is only so
that you might see more clearly where we have
strayed and might come to carry us home.

Ezekiel 34:11–12, 15–17
Psalm 23
1 Corinthians 15:20–26, 28
Matthew 25:31–46

*When he looked up he saw some wealthy people putting
their offerings into the treasury and he noticed a poor
widow putting in two small coins. He said, "I tell you
truly, this poor widow put in more than all the rest; for
those others have all made offerings from their surplus
wealth, but she, from her poverty, has offered her whole
livelihood."*

— LUKE 21:1–4

It cost Eric nearly a tenth of his salary to keep
his invalid mother in the nursing home. It cost
Gerry his health and his strength, his freedom
and his life to keep his invalid mother at home.

Revelation 14:1–5
Psalm 24
Luke 21:1–4

NOVEMBER 26

All that you see here—the days will come when there will not be left a stone upon another stone that will not be thrown down.

— LUKE 21:6

When I look around me at all the things, places, and people that I cherish and then imagine the empty space that would remain were I to lose them all, I begin to grasp the extent of my need and the depth of your love, which alone can fill my need.

.Revelation 14:14–19
Psalm 96
Luke 21:5–11

*They will seize and persecute you, they will hand you over
to the synagogues and to prisons, and they will have you
led before kings and governors because of my name. It will
lead to your giving testimony.*

— LUKE 21:12–13

When they make fun of us, Lord, because of our
faith, we have a choice: we can feel sorry for
ourselves, or we can feel proud of you.

Revelation 15:1–4
Psalm 98
Luke 21:12–19

There will be signs in the sun, the moon, and the stars, and on earth nations will be in dismay, perplexed by the roaring of the sea and the waves. People will die of fright in anticipation of what is coming upon the world, for the powers of the heavens will be shaken. . . . But when these signs begin to happen, stand erect and raise your heads because your redemption is at hand.

— LUKE 21:25 – 26, 28

The same earthquake that shatters our homes also breaks open our prisons. The same turmoil that rocks our certainties also shakes free the chains around our hearts.

Revelation 18:1–2, 21–23; 19:1–3, 9
Psalm 100
Luke 21:20–28

My soul yearns and pines
for the courts of the LORD.

— PSALM 84:3

My desires are the proof that my heart knows
that there is something beyond me. My longings
dislodge my heart from my self and draw it
toward the possibility of you.

Revelation 20:1–4, 11–21:2
Psalm 84
Luke 21:29–33

As he was walking by the Sea of Galilee, he saw two brothers, Simon who is called Peter, and his brother Andrew, casting a net into the sea; they were fishermen. He said to them, "Come after me, and I will make you fishers of men." At once they left their nets and followed him.

— MATTHEW 4:18–20

The personal skills with which we earn our living become, under your leadership, the specific gifts with which you call us to use to bless creation with your loving.

Romans 10:9–18
Psalm 19
Matthew 4:18–22

We have all withered like leaves,
and our guilt carries us away like the wind.

— ISAIAH 64:5

Out in the garden the fallen leaves settle like a blanket over the withered grass. It looks as desolate as my own storm-swept heart so often feels, yet I know that this blanket of fallenness is covering and sheltering the unborn seeds of springtime.

Isaiah 63:16–17, 19; 64:2–7
Psalm 80
1 Corinthians 1:3–9
Mark 13:33–37

O house of Jacob, come,
let us walk in the light of the LORD!

— ISAIAH 2:5

I closed my book and turned out the light. It was
then that I noticed the night sky, bright with
starlight. As long as the light in my room was
burning, all I could see was my room and its
messy contents. But when I turned out the light
and refocused my gaze on what lay outside and
beyond me, my vision was drawn out to a reality
far beyond myself and infinitely greater.

Isaiah 2:1–5
Psalm 122
Matthew 8:5–11

DECEMBER 3

• SAINT FRANCIS XAVIER, PRIEST •

There shall be no harm or ruin on all my holy mountain;
for the earth shall be filled with knowledge of the LORD,
as water covers the sea.

— ISAIAH 11:9

The gently rising tide crept imperceptibly up
the beach, gradually freeing stranded sea
creatures and dried-up seaweed from the desert
wastes of ebb tide, and what had at first seemed
like a fear-inspiring invasion of the unknown
revealed itself to be a flood tide of new life and
grace and fruitfulness.

Isaiah 11:1–10
Psalm 72
Luke 10:21–24

"Let us rejoice and be glad that he has saved us!"
For the hand of the LORD will rest on this mountain.

— ISAIAH 25:9–10

The mountain of anxieties and resistances in my
heart and in my life seemed insurmountable
until, in the quiet of prayer, you rested your
hand of blessing upon it. From then on, however
harsh the terrain, it became the mountain where
I had met you, and a place of joy and gratitude.

Isaiah 25:6–10
Psalm 23
Matthew 15:29–37

Open the gates of victory;
I will enter and thank the LORD.

— PSALM 118:19

You open the gates of your presence to us in the silence of our individual prayer, but when we go through those gates, we find ourselves in the heart of the hurts and the needs of our brothers and sisters.

Isaiah 26:1–6
Psalm 118
Matthew 7:21, 24–27

On that day the deaf shall hear
the words of a book;
And out of gloom and darkness,
the eyes of the blind shall see.

— ISAIAH 29:18

I didn't hear the sound of your crying because I
was tuned in to my own regrets. I didn't see your
hand outstretched in need because my eyes were
blinded by my own resentments. Forgive me,
friend, and let me try again.

Isaiah 29:17–24
Psalm 27
Matthew 9:27–31

The Lord will give you the bread you need
and the water for which you thirst.
No longer will your Teacher hide himself,
but with your own eyes you shall see your Teacher. . . .
He will give rain for the seed
that you sow in the ground,
And the wheat that the soil produces
will be rich and abundant.

— ISAIAH 30:20, 23

The bread that we make from the seeds of our
sorrow will sustain us more truly and more
completely than the sweet cakes of our fleeting
pleasures can.

Isaiah 30:19–21, 23–26
Psalm 147
Matthew 9:35–10:1, 6–8

A voice of one crying out in the desert:
"Prepare the way of the Lord,
make straight his paths."

— MARK 1:3

In the good times, when my life's music is playing at top volume, I hear no voice except my own. But when I am lost and bewildered, a new voice breaks through the wilderness of my heart, calling me to take just one more step along the path that will lead me home.

Isaiah 40:1–5, 9–11
Psalm 85
2 Peter 3:8–14
Mark 1:1–8

Do not be afraid, Mary, for you have found favor with God. Behold, you will conceive in your womb and bear a son, and you shall name him Jesus.

— LUKE 1:30 – 31

For our journey with God, the only word we need to learn is *yes*.

Genesis 3:9–15, 20
Psalm 98
Ephesians 1:3–6, 11–12
Luke 1:26–38

DECEMBER 10

A voice cries out:
In the desert prepare the way of the LORD!
Make straight in the wasteland a highway for our God!

— ISAIAH 40:3

In the gardens of my life my path meanders
around every delightful distraction, but my
desert paths lead me straight to you.

Isaiah 40:1–11
Psalm 96
Matthew 18:12–14

They that hope in the LORD will renew their strength,
they will soar as with eagles' wings;
They will run and not grow weary,
walk and not grow faint.

— ISAIAH 40:31

When I am doing those things that satisfy my heart's deepest desires, I discover that they generate a new energy within me that leaves me with enough to fuel the necessary tasks that I would rather not do at all.

Isaiah 40:25–31
Psalm 103
Matthew 11:28–30

DECEMBER 12

When Elizabeth heard Mary's greeting, the infant leaped in her womb, and Elizabeth, filled with the holy Spirit, cried out in a loud voice.

— LUKE 1:41–42

It was hard settling into the new neighborhood. Judy and Ross felt like unwelcome outsiders. But that all changed when Sue dropped by with some flowers and some homemade jam. "Great to have you here," she told them. And somewhere deep inside them, new life leaped for joy.

Zechariah 2:14–17 or Revelation 11:19; 12:1–6, 10
Psalm 45
Luke 1:26–38 or 1:39–47 or any readings from the
Common of the Blessed Virgin Mary, nos. 707–712

• SAINT LUCY, VIRGIN AND MARTYR •

Thus says the LORD, your redeemer,
the Holy One of Israel:
I, the LORD, your God,
teach you what is for your good,
and lead you on the way you should go.

— ISAIAH 48:17

In a world where every demand and pressure
seems to drive us, may we know your love,
which meets us where we are and leads us gently
toward our own deepest truth in you.

Isaiah 48:17–19
Psalm 1
Matthew 11:16–19

Till like a fire there appeared the prophet
whose words were as a flaming furnace.

— SIRACH 48:1

Your word, too, Lord, touches our lives as a
furnace would, burning away our masks and
pretenses yet kindling the steady candle of your
leading love in our hearts.

Sirach 48:1–4, 9–11
Psalm 80
Matthew 17:10–13

A man came, sent by God.
His name was John.
He came as a witness,
as a witness to speak for that Light
so that everyone might believe through him.
He was not the Light, only a witness to speak for the Light.

— JOHN 1:6 – 8

We are not called to be lights ourselves but to be windowpanes through which your light might shine on others.

Isaiah 61:1–2, 10–11
Luke 1:46–50, 53–54
1 Thessalonians 5:16–24
John 1:6–8, 19–28

Good and upright is the LORD,
who shows sinners the way,
Guides the humble rightly,
and teaches the humble the way.

— PSALM 25:8 – 9

The map was useless. The directions I had been
given made no sense when I was lost. Then a
friendly companion came up next to me: "I'll
come with you and show you the way," he said.
And I knew that I had met you, my Lord and
guide, in the maze of my life and that your way
of leading me is to walk the way with me.

Numbers 24:2–7, 15–17
Psalm 25
Matthew 21:23–27

DECEMBER 17

Assemble and listen, sons of Jacob,
listen to Israel, your father.

— GENESIS 49:2

When we tune out the noise of our lives, we
begin to discover the deep vibrations of silence,
revealing the innermost movements of our
hearts.

Genesis 49:2, 8–10
Psalm 72
Matthew 1:1–17

All this took place to fulfill what the Lord had said through the prophet:
"Behold, the virgin shall be with child and bear a son,
and they shall name him Emmanuel,"
which means "God is with us."

— MATTHEW 1:22 – 23

I walked the pilgrim paths, seeking you in the shrines of the faithful. I climbed the mountain paths, seeking you in the wonders of creation. I ventured down the hidden pathways of my heart, and I found you in every moment of my lived experience. God is with us—in our faith, in our world, and in our living.

Jeremiah 23:5–8
Psalm 72
Matthew 1:18–24

DECEMBER 19

Both [Zechariah and Elizabeth] were righteous in the eyes of God, observing all the commandments and ordinances of the Lord blamelessly. But they had no child, because Elizabeth was barren and both were advanced in years.

— LUKE 1:6–7

We can keep our lives in order by observing the law and doing what is right, but only love will make them fruitful.

Judges 13:2–7, 24–25
Psalm 71
Luke 1:5–25

*The holy Spirit will come upon you, and the power of the
Most High will overshadow you.*

— LUKE 1:35

When your presence touches our lives, it comes
gently and silently, covering us with yourself, as
a loving mother covers her child at bedtime, as
the snow covers the frozen earth, incubating the
springtime.

Isaiah 7:10–14
Psalm 24
Luke 1:26–38

Saturday

DECEMBER 21

For see, the winter is past,
the rains are over and gone.
The flowers appear on the earth.
— SONG OF SONGS 2:11–12

Open our eyes, Lord, so that we may see, every day, one little sign of life, of hope, of resurrection as we walk through the dark rainy days of our souls' winter. And open our lips, so that we may share the joy of our discovery with someone else who needs to hear it.

Song of Songs 2:8–14 or Zephaniah 3:14–18
Psalm 33
Luke 1:39–45

DECEMBER 22

• FOURTH SUNDAY OF ADVENT •

And behold, Elizabeth, your relative, has also conceived a
son in her old age, and this is the sixth month for her who
was called barren; for nothing will be impossible for God.

— LUKE 1:36 – 37

We will discover that the most barren places of
our experience are often pregnant with our
deepest truths if we will only wait and watch, in
patient trust, for their gestation.

2 Samuel 7:1–5, 8–12, 14, 16
Psalm 89
Romans 16:25–27
Luke 1:26–38

When they came on the eighth day to circumcise the child,
they were going to call him Zechariah after his father, but
his mother said in reply, "No. He will be called John." . . .
[The father] asked for a tablet and wrote, "John is his name."

— LUKE 1:59–60, 63

Our name is the welcome gift we receive from
our human parents, an identity to grow into.
Our true identity for all eternity is the welcome
gift you promise us when we enter your
kingdom.

Malachi 3:1–4, 23–24
Psalm 25
Luke 1:57–66

DECEMBER 24

*And you, child, will be called prophet of the Most High,
for you will go before the Lord to prepare his ways.*

— LUKE 1:76

Road making is hard work. It leaves us bruised
and exhausted. When we feel like this in our
attempts to serve you, Lord, remind us whose
way it is that we are building.

2 Samuel 7:1–5, 8–12, 14, 16
Psalm 89
Luke 1:67–79

DECEMBER 25

• CHRISTMAS • THE NATIVITY OF THE LORD •

The people who walked in darkness
have seen a great light;
Upon those who dwelt in the land of gloom
a light has shone.

— ISAIAH 9:1

In the darkness all I can see are the Christmas lights twinkling on the tree in the garden. But when the dawn breaks, the whole tree will be alive with the light of the rising sun, and the twinkling fairy lights will be eclipsed by the light of day.

*But beware of people, for they will hand you over to courts
and scourge you in their synagogues, and you will be led
before governors and kings for my sake.*

— MATTHEW 10:17–18

The tender vulnerability of the Christ child
walks hand in hand with the raw forces that lead
him to Calvary. Your way will not protect us
against opposition and hostility, but it will give
us the strength to live through it and move
beyond it.

Acts 6:8–10; 7:54–59
Psalm 31
Matthew 10:17–22

Friday

DECEMBER 27

[W]hat we have seen and heard
we proclaim now to you,
so that you too may have fellowship with us.

—1 JOHN 1:3

What we have to tell is not something we have
been taught or something we have read in
books, but a living stream flowing from our own
experience of the power of your presence.

1 John 1:1–4
Psalm 97
John 20:2–8

⇒ 401 ⇐

A voice was heard in Ramah,
sobbing and loud lamentation;
Rachel weeping for her children,
and she would not be consoled,
since they were no more.

— MATTHEW 2:18

May we never cease to cry out with all our energy against the harm we suffer and the harm we do, until your justice flows through every nation, every family, and every human heart.

1 John 1:5–2:2
Psalm 124
Matthew 2:13–18

Let the word of Christ dwell in you richly.

— COLOSSIANS 3:16

Your message, Lord, is like a growing embryo. It begins as a single seed in my heart, and it grows and swells until my heart is too small to contain it. Then it lives a life of its own, carrying my life within it.

Sirach 3:2–7, 12–14 or Genesis 15:1–6; 21:1–3
Psalm 128
Colossians 3:12–21 or 3:12–17 or Hebrews 11:8, 11–12, 17–19
Luke 2:22–40 or 2:22, 39–40

Yet the world and its enticement are passing away. But whoever does the will of God remains forever.

—1 JOHN 2:17

The children had spent a boisterous Christmas Day unwrapping their toys, playing with them, and then discarding them in search of new excitement. At bedtime, they cried over the anticlimax. Cuddled up in their parents' arms, they at last found something that would never grow stale.

1 John 2:12–17
Psalm 96
Luke 2:36–40

DECEMBER 31

• NEW YEAR'S EVE • SAINT SYLVESTER I, POPE •

In the beginning was the Word,
and the Word was with God,
and the Word was God.

— JOHN 1:1

Tomorrow is a new beginning. And every moment we live for the rest of our lives is a new beginning. Let every moment, therefore, become a space into which God can speak his creating word, and let our whole lives become carriers of his meaning and his truth.

1 John 2:18–21
Psalm 96
John 1:1–18